BRIDGING THE GAP

Second Edition

A Parent's Guide

Terry J. Walker, M.A.

A Gap Closer™ Publication

All Rights Reserved.
Copyright © 2014 by Terry J. Walker, M.A.
Cover Design © 2014 by Terry J. Walker, M.A.
Back Cover Photography © by Margie King Photography
Cover Photography © 2014 by Debbie Neely Photography
IAM Logo by Debbie Neely Photography
Edited by Dr. Angela D. Massey

Copyright © 2014 by Terry J. Walker, M.A. All Rights Reserved. Printed in the United States of America. Except as permitted under the United States Copyright Act of 1976, no part of this book may be reproduced in any form or by any electronic or mechanical means including information storage and retrieval systems—except in the case of brief quotations in articles or reviews—without the prior written permission of its publisher, Life on Purpose Publishing and/or Terry J. Walker, M.A.
All brand names and product names used in this book are trademarks, registered trademarks, or trade names of their respective holders
ISBN: 0-9729250-6-6
ISBN-13: 978-0-9729250-6-8

This publication is designed to provide accurate and authoritative information in regard to the subject matter covered. It is sold with the understanding that neither the publisher nor the author is not engaged in rendering legal or other professional services. If legal advice or other expert assistance is required, the services of a competent professional person should be sought.

—From a declaration of principles jointly adopted by a committee of the American Bar Association and a committee of publishers.

A Gap Closer ™ Publication
       A Division of Life On Purpose Publishing
       Windsor, Connecticut

Dedication

(To Braxton)

Thank you for allowing me to have first-hand knowledge of what juggling a career and parenthood is all about. Thank you for all the joy and laughter you have brought to my life. I am grateful that you came in my life at the right time and the right reason, and I am honored to call you son. Thank you for teaching me how to bend and to understand the importance of allowing our children to find and enhance their own creativity and passion.

Praises for Bridging The Gap, First Ed.

"I am certainly impressed with the training program you have established called "Bridging the Gap." I believe it is important to have parental involvement during the education of each child. This program microscopes that need." *Former Tennessee Senator Lincoln Davis*

"Bridging The Gap" is a program which we can all point to with great pride!!" *Former Tennessee State Senator Anna Belle Clement O'Brien*

"Your approach hits at the core of this problem and is an excellent strategy to get parents involved. By 'Bridging the Gap' between educators, children, and families, the education process will be enhanced." *Mr. Jim Purcell, Past Director, Tennessee Technology Center*

"I want to commend you on your development of "Bridging The Gap." To develop better communication between families and educators is an excellent concept. I am certain your experience in developing and implementing treatment strategies for at risk youth has given you exceptional insight into early intervention in the lives of children." *Nancy B. Carman, Former Asst. Vice Chancellor for Instruction Tennessee Board of Regents*

Acknowledgements

Thank you to my parents for supporting me through my writing endeavors and for allowing me to reach for my dreams.

Thank you to my grandparents for loving and supporting me. Although you are not here in the physical sense, I still believe you are with me every day.

I especially want to thank all of the families and children I have had the opportunity to work with over the years. We have encountered successes and pitfalls, but no matter the case, we continued to keep working, teaching, learning, growing and moving forward.

Thank you to Deb for believing in this project back in the early days and for your willingness to support me.

Thank you to *all* my friends both past and present who have supported my "crazy" ideas (even if they tried to run the other way), but stood beside me on this one.

Thank you Beth P. for your help and support when I first began this project. Although you aren't here to see it come to life, I know you are laughing and shaking your head as I continue to say: "I got an idea!"

Thank you to Vicki for reminding me that I did make a difference and for supporting me through revitalizing this project and bringing it back to life.

Thank you to a wonderful therapist and friend, Cindy C., who always knew I would "write this book!"

Thank you, Debbie, for your creative skills and abilities on the photography and also for your impeccable advice for IAM. You came along at the right time and for the right reasons and I am so very grateful for all your help and support. I look forward to our continued growth, my friend.

Thank you to my editor and friend: Dr. Angela Massey. We have laughed, we have cried and we have buckled down to "get the job done." I'm so grateful for you, and yes, I know... "you got me!"

Contents

Acknowledgements	vii
Introduction	xiii
1 Understanding Child Development	1
2 Understanding Adulthood and Parenting	13
3 Dealing with Feelings (Including Grief and Loss)	23
4 Establishing Rapport and Self-Esteem	35
5 Coping Skills	45
6 Communication and Listening Skills	53
7 Warning Signs of Abuse and Bullying	63
8 Parent and Educator Involvement	75
9 Love and Respect vs. Obey and Control	83
10 Wants vs. Needs	91
11 Natural and Logical Consequences	97

BRIDGING THE GAP

Second Edition

A Parent's Guide

Introduction

This book is designed to enhance your child's behavioral skills and educational abilities. Bridging The Gap, A Parent's Guide, is the second phase of the program that intends to help "bridge the gap" between children, educators, and families. The plan for this program is based on two phases: A program for daycare, head start and early-childhood educators, and a book for parents and families. The book and the program proposes an opportunity for everyone to work together to help our children gain a better understanding of themselves. The book also provides information to help us as adults to look at our own behaviors and gain an understanding of how we may be perceived—not only by other adults, but also by our own children. In today's fast-paced society, children are being raised in homes where both parents have to work full-time or in a single-family home in which that parent works full-time in an attempt to make ends meet. This program has evolved from my years of working with children and families for over 15 years in various therapeutic settings and have taken the working family into great consideration from which this book has evolved.

We are seeing a continuous increase in violence and various types of abuse among our children today. There has also been an increase in family stress related to the changes in the workforce and trying to maintain a home. After working all day, the family picks up their child from daycare or school, goes home, puts supper on, bathes the child and then goes to bed, only to start the next day over again. Most daycare programs provide a service to keep your child safe.

In today's school system, the teacher barely has enough time to ensure that your child's educational goals are met in each subject.

What's missing? Quality time and efforts to enhance a child's basic emotional needs! I believe that if a child has not obtained the necessary behavioral and emotional skills needed in everyday life (what a lot of adults take for granted), then he or she will have emotional barriers to both personal and educational growth. Because I want parents, educators, and children to benefit from this book, it is based on simplicity and fun.

We are entering a time in which people are having to accept change within their careers and personal lives. This is a time of spiritual awareness and positive growth for everyone in our society. We are looking toward the need for world peace and becoming aware of the fact that some of our children have strayed from the "beaten path." It is a time for growth and change, both internally and externally. It is a time for education, knowledge, love, and acceptance. This is the time to take back our lives and help our families to unite and grow. It is time to take off our blinders, ask questions, and look for answers to what is happening around us.

If *Bridging the Gap* benefits one family, child, or educator to change the way they handle specific situations in a more effective and positive manner, then it has served its purpose. It is written in everyday language and is not to be made difficult in any way. That is the foundation for this program and this book, therefore, let's work together toward *bridging the gap*.

Namaste!

Terry J. Walker, M.A.
Nashville, Tennessee

1 Understanding Child Development

Before we begin, we must first understand where your child may be in his or her developmental stage. As I stated in the introduction, this is written in everyday language and is an overview in gaining an understanding of childhood development. It is not medical terminology, but is based on brief facts and tidbits for you to understand better where your child may be developmentally.

A child between the ages of 4 – 6 begins to think of the world in terms of *self*, and is unable to appreciate someone else's perspective on things. (Makes you wonder if some adults ever grew out of this stage.) They are also unable to understand how to accept responsibility for their own behaviors. This is also the time when you may hear the question "why?" quite often. To help decrease your own personal frustration, during this stage keep in mind that providing brief and simple answers that the child can understand will increase his or her awareness and hopefully lessen the continuous "why?" question. The phrase, "because I said," does not educate a child nor does it satisfy a child's curiosity. You don't have to give a long-drawn-out explanation, just one that the child can understand and trust.

On the positive side, your child should be gaining an understanding of classifying objects into categories, such as shapes, colors, letters, and numbers. At this time, a child's short-term memory is increasing along with his or her attention span and language development. An average 4-year-old should exhibit an increasing vocabulary and begin to show improvement in using word sequence appropriately in sentences and by asking questions. Children in this age group have what we call "concrete thinking." I'm sure you've heard the phrase, "the grass isn't always greener on the other side of the fence." If you say something like this to a child, you will leave that child wondering what fence you're talking about, where that fence is, and what color is the grass if it's not green. What we as adults take for granted in our daily conversations may leave a child dazed and confused. To minimize frustration for both you and the child, keep answers simple, and make sure the child understands what you are telling him or her. Take a moment in your conversation to allow your child to respond to you about what was heard and understood. Furthermore, take the time to understand and be clear on what your child is trying to explain to you. Building and establishing open communication is imperative during these years.

During this developmental stage, your child's relationship with you is more important than peer relationships. This is a very important time to grasp and build a healthy, emotional and trusting relationship with your child! Working with your child on self-esteem and socialization skills are of utmost importance during this period. In addition, in this stage of development, your child will begin to gain an awareness of gender identity.

As a parent, it is important for you to monitor and educate your child regarding cooperative, healthy play and group skills. If you spend quality time with your child, he or she might just teach you a thing or two. In this developmental stage, as in the following stages, you should be aware of the types of influences your child is exposed to, for example:

- What is your child watching on television?
- What kind of music is he or she listening to?
- What types of books are they reading?

- What types of video games are they interested in playing?
- What are their social media outlets of choice?

You must also be aware of the friendships they are beginning to establish and their peer interactions. The earlier you, as a parent, begin to listen and become actively involved in your child's life, the better rapport you will have established. Again, this is a very important time for building and maintaining open communication and trust.

Your child also needs to know you will not respond in anger when mistakes are made; rather, you will talk through things together and gain a better awareness and understanding. Mistakes provide lessons for growth. What you role model during this time is how your child will learn and grow. If your child thinks you will respond in anger, then you instill fear and shut down all forms of effective communication. If your child knows you will help them understand and learn from a situation, and that you are not angry, then he or she will be more prone to listening, trusting and learning from you.

The next stage of development is that of middle to late childhood from ages seven to puberty. The child will begin to show steady physical growth, weight gain, and better coordination. The child should also begin to show improvement in his or her motor skills. The child's attention span begins to increase during this time, as well their ability to process, and organize information. Parents need to maintain consistency in daily schedules. This is a great time to establish and maintain a rule, consequence, and reward system within the family. Keep in mind that I said a rule, consequence, *and* reward system. Often times we get caught up in the fact that when a rule is broken, we suffer the consequence. This becomes a way of life: if you break a rule, then you suffer the consequence. But what if the child follows directions and doesn't break rules? Or what if the child regularly does the chores? Do we recognize those attributes and reward behaviors on a consistent basis?

As adults, we have a tendency to take things for granted. As long as things run smoothly, we ignore other benefits such as consistent rewards and praise. It becomes an expectation to do well with no semblance of reward or acknowledgement or praise. As an adult, if you consistently show up for work on time each day and do a good job, or possibly go beyond your job description to do other things or to help others, wouldn't you appreciate acknowledgement, praise and possibly a raise and/or a promotion? If you don't receive praise or rewards from your boss or company, then your productivity will likely decrease and/or you will begin to look for another job. Keep this example in mind when your child is following your household rules and going to school each day. We all need motivation, love, praise and acceptance. If we do not receive these things, then we begin to ask: "What's the point in doing it if there is nothing positive to receive?"

During this stage of development, it is important to help your child to understand how to accept responsibility for his or her behaviors and to show more responsibility in regard to educational activities and household chores. This is also a good time to help your child develop interests in hobbies, sports, or other related activities. Socialization and peer relationships will begin to take shape during this stage.

This is a great time to help your child enhance his or her interests, creativity and skills. We all have things we are interested in and passionate about; take this time to help your child begin to find their passion and enhance their skills and abilities. Observe their activities and interests and help them to develop them. Don't try to steer them in a direction you *think* they should go based on your own motives and interests. Allow them to find their own interests, their own creativity and be supportive of them.

Everyone cannot be a football star or famous gymnast based on a parent's opinion for their child. These types of expectations put undue pressure on the child for something the parent wants. Eventually, they will lead to negativity or failure or the feeling of not being good enough. We all have something we are passionate about and skills we can explore and develop. As a parent, you should help your child to recognize his or her creative skills and help to develop and enhance those skills.

The final stage of childhood development is the dreaded adolescence stage. The child's body continues to grow and develop physically along with the internal hormonal changes that begin to take place in both males and females. During this stage of development, it is important that your child gains a healthy perspective on their feelings and behaviors. This includes educational awareness of what is happening with their bodies. This is also the time to educate your child on the importance of abstinence, contraceptives, and sexually transmitted diseases.

Unfortunately, exposure to alcohol, drugs, and sex is predominant among our children and society today. If we bury our heads in the sand, it will not go away, and it will not stop children from experimenting or being exposed to it. Realize that children will be exposed to these things and—to use a cliché—"the best defense is a good offense." Your offense is to educate, educate, educate. You need to keep an open line of communication between you and your child.

The adolescent also needs further education on how to establish and maintain healthy relationships within both same and opposite gender groups. As a parent, remember that with alcohol, drugs, sex, and peer pressure being so prevalent among our teens today, it is very difficult to help them establish a positive identity and high self-esteem if it was not provided to them during the childhood years.

During the adolescent period, the parent can expect conflict over various issues in the adolescent's life. The adolescent is attempting to become more autonomous. At this stage, peer relationships begin to override parent-child relationships. Alcohol, drug, and sexual experimentation are prevalent among peer groups. At this time, it becomes very important that you and your adolescent have already established a trusting, positive, open line of communication. If it was established during the early childhood years, you and your teenager can work together through this phase of adolescence. It is also an important time to maintain an awareness of what is going on in your child's life. I have worked with so many families that say, "I wanted to give my child his or her privacy, and never went in his or her room to even have a conversation," or "Entering my child's room would invade his or her privacy." There are many adolescents in hospitals today because of this privacy misconception by the parents. On the other hand, the adolescents report that their parents "don't care about them" or "didn't spend any time with them." Many of these adolescents feel they have been left to try to figure things out on their own.

I feel adolescence is a confusing time for the teen; it is also confusing for the parent. As a parent, consider some of the following questions:

- How can a parent talk to the teen if the teen doesn't want to talk to the parent? The teenager comes in from school, goes to his or her room, and shuts the door. Nowadays, they likely get on the phone, text or interact through social media. The parent's *thinking* is that the teen needs to be alone or needs *privacy.*
- As a parent, do you continue to let your teenager shut him/herself off from the family or do you continue to let the teen know you are there if he or she needs to talk?
- Do you readily make yourself available and maintain some type of family function, even if it's just eating dinner as a family a couple of times a week, turning off the television or other outside distractions and having a discussion?
- If you are having discussions, have they become one sided where you do all the talking or harping on the teen?
- Do you provide open lines of communication and make efforts to do things with your teen and to support your teen?
- Do you allow friends to come over? Do you have an active role of communication with your child and their friends? You can find out a lot about your child and their friends if you allow for open communication and interaction. Have a cookout, provide interactive games and opportunities to communicate and have fun. This builds trust with you and your child along with their friends.

I have found with teens if you invite them into the living room, sit down and try to have a conversation it usually does not work. This is a forceful energy action based on expectations and will usually lead to a counter force of energy or a push back from the teen. It puts undo pressure on everyone involved and will only lead to further frustration. Clearly, it accomplishes nothing. Most likely, it leads to further frustration on both the part of the parent and the teen.

On the other hand, I have also found that if you make an effort to do something with the teen that provides some type of interaction or fun—whether it's going for a walk, going for a drive, throwing a ball, playing a game, etc.—it seems to provide an opportunity to help open up lines of communication. Once you begin to engage in an activity of sorts, communication is no longer forced and can flow easily. This is a great time to listen to what is being said and what is *not* being said. You might even ask a few questions. It is imperative that you remain calm and open. If the teen feels you getting agitated or angry, then he or she will likely shut down and feel as though you cannot be trusted or confided in.

During this stage of development, you need to know that if a healthy bond was not established during the time your child depended on you as a parent, it will be much more difficult to establish a bond when the child is going through adolescence. While it is more difficult, it is not impossible. As you know, it is difficult to build a house by starting with the walls and placing a roof if you have not established a foundation. However, you can always begin to build or reestablish a foundation and trust with your teen, but you must be willing to put forth consistent, positive effort.

The leading causes of death among teenagers are accidents, murder, and suicide. Primarily, this is related to alcohol and drug usage. In today's society, teens are under a great deal of peer pressure, and as adults, we should not rule out the possibility of depression becoming a factor in our child's life. Keep in mind their body is going through many changes. Their hormones are becoming more prevalent, which causes moodiness; socially, they feel awkward about themselves. Along with peer pressure, we need to be aware of the child's self-induced pressure to succeed in grades, sports, or become a part of a group and trying to fit in. As the parent, you also need to consider your own behaviors and how much pressure you may be applying on your own child to do better or to be or act a certain way. If you combine all these outside pressures, they can become overwhelming to the teen.

Bridging the Gap is the foundation to work with your child during the early years to establish a positive sense of self and goals to help get through the adolescent years. This is not "a be all, end all" book to perfect parenting or teaching, but is filled with ideas and information for you as the parent to be more creative in raising and establishing a healthy, lasting, and trusting bond with your child.

Each person responds differently to different structures and dynamics. The important concept to remember is that you are the parent, the teacher, and the role model for your child. Children learn by watching. How you cope and respond to certain situations is how your child will learn and mimic your behaviors. Behavior is learned, and you have become the teacher. If you want your child to learn to accept responsibility for his or her actions, then it begins with you role modeling that type of behavior. If you want respect, you must respect yourself and give respect to others. The days of "do as I say, not as I do" need to become a statement of the past for you and your family. I recognize that people and families are different, and the entire book may not fit your every need, but take what you can, be creative, and use it to your advantage.

The work force is changing rapidly and so must society and our role in it. Government and corporations have placed more stress on people to work harder and possibly longer hours just to remain employed. With this concept, families and family dynamics have gone by the wayside in an effort to maintain a home and pay bills. We find ourselves in a world of working all the time and always striving but never arriving. We go to work, come home, put supper on the table and everyone goes their separate ways. We spend our evening upset from the day's events or complaining about the day's work and allow it to consume our evening as well. We seem to find ourselves in a game of always playing "catch up." We must get back to nurturing our families and ourselves, or we will continue to remain as a hamster on a wheel and always running to keep up and never really accomplishing anything. We lose our sense of self in this dynamic, and we lose our sense of family.

Social media has become more prevalent these days and is used as an outlet or pastime for our children and ourselves. However, it can also become detrimental to the entire family. We now have "sexting," along with children being exposed to unhealthy and possibly incomplete or inaccurate information on the Internet or through their friends.

Bullying is now a huge factor in schools, and violence is becoming rampant both in schools and through social media. We have started to live in fear for our children to go to school. School is supposed to be a safe place for our children to grow and to learn without the worry of being bullied, beaten or even killed. We must learn to take back our lives and our families and become more aware of what is going on around us. Otherwise, we are allowing outside negative influences and forces to run our lives and the lives of our families. Whether those outside forces or influences come in the form of job dissatisfaction, social media, violent video games, sex, drugs, etc., we must become aware of these influences and work to educate ourselves about them. You've heard the statement: "knowledge is power," you must begin to be more aware of your life and actions and what you wish to represent, along with educating yourself on the influences your children are exposed to. We must be positive, strong and help our children have a bright, productive future. This includes changes in family dynamics and building trust and open communication. This includes putting ourselves first, nurturing ourselves and nurturing our families. I hope that this book benefits you and your family in a multitude of ways, and I wish you well in your parenting endeavors!

2 Understanding Adulthood and Parenting

After gaining an awareness of where your child may be in his or her developmental stage it is necessary for you, the parent, to gain an understanding of where you are in your own life. To establish true change, each individual must begin with self. It is also important that you understand your own strengths and weaknesses. If you don't deal with and accept who you are as an individual, how do you expect your child to gain a better awareness of him- or herself? Unfortunately, when the stork arrived, it failed to bring a list of instructions to help you raise your child. One thing I do know, you opted to take on a parental role. The responsibility of that role requires a constant awareness of where you are in both your personal and professional life. This may be a difficult chapter for you, but it is imperative to have an understanding of where you are in your life so that you can teach and role model a positive, productive, educational life for your child.

Family dynamics—both past and present—impact how you intend to raise your child. Most of us, at one time or another, have heard or even said, "I'm not going to raise my children the way my parents raised me." Whether your parents were the best parents or the worst parents, unless you identify the cycles in your own family dynamics that you do not wish to repeat, you will likely make similar choices and decisions. The following are some examples of various family dynamics that I have encountered with families I have worked with over the years. Take a moment to consider the following and recognize if you or someone you know may fall into any of these categories while growing up or are currently living out this family dynamic:

- Family of high achievers and possibly "workaholics"
    - Do you feel your family had time for you or spent quality time with you?
    - Did your family set unrealistic or high expectation goals for you?
    - Are you currently setting unrealistic expectations on yourself, your partner or your children?
- Family abused alcohol and/or drugs
    - Do you abuse alcohol and/or drugs?
    - Have you married or do you live with someone who abuses alcohol and/or drugs?
- Family exhibited domestic violence or other types of abuse
    - Did you or your partner grow up in this type of household?
    - Do you and your partner have "knock down, drag out arguments"?
    - Do your children witness or hear these arguments?
    - Are you married to or live with someone who is violent, aggressive, argumentative, abusive, and negative?
    - Are you easily angered, aggressive, or negative?

Ask yourself the above questions and answer them honestly. There are no right or wrong answers to these questions and you're the only one who knows the answers. As you answer the questions and become more honest with yourself, keep in mind that change begins from within and begins with each individual person. Ignoring this information does not make it go away. This is the opportunity for you to recognize this information and to make the first step in a more positive direction for yourself and your family. You must recognize that history does repeat itself and for the more difficult lessons, we will continue to repeat or fall into the same cycles until we recognize and understand the patterns before we can change them.

With the families I have worked with over the years, one common theme seems to arise: "It's not my child!" "My child wouldn't have done this or been involved if it wasn't for that little _____ (fill in the blank) down the street!" "It's not my child, it's that bunch he or she's been hanging with!" I've heard these and similar phrases over the years. The common theme comes down to the simple fact that no one wants to accept responsibility for themselves or for the actions of their child. My provocative question was: "Well, if it's not your child doing these things, and it wasn't the child whose family was here in this office before you, then whose child is it?" Apparently, there must be a child or teenager out there that has started a 'snowball or ripple effect' and has been the single cause for all youngsters to get into trouble. If we could just find this one particular child, then everybody's problems will be solved. *(Sarcasm intended!)*

No one wants their child to have emotional, educational or physical problems but the fact that we are all human makes it likely for issues to occur in any of these three forms. In the work force, most of us do not like it when someone shifts the responsibility and we end up doing his or her work along with our own. For example, if our supervisor is called on the carpet with their boss. Well, you know the rest about how it "rolls downhill." When the buck is passed down, it may not seem so great anymore. Many of us can easily place blame on others or events and make excuses for our behaviors and actions. On the other hand, when we become the recipient of blame or anger we certainly don't like it. By taking into consideration, as a parent, employee, co-worker, etc., we must begin to accept responsibility for our own behaviors and actions. If we don't start to accept responsibility for our own behaviors and role model that behavior for our children, how can we expect our children to learn how to accept responsibility for their actions? After all, as adults, parents, and educators, we are the role models and the teachers. If we role model behaviors such as not accepting responsibility for our choices and our actions, then how do we expect our children to learn to accept responsibility for their choices and actions? How do we help them to make wiser choices?

As I stated in Chapter 1, the middle to late childhood stage of development is an optimum time to begin actively teaching your child how to accept responsibility for his/her own behaviors and implementing a choices-consequences-rewards system within the family. However, the earlier you begin working with your child on awareness of responsibility for his/her own actions, the better. As the parent, you should know when your child is able to start grasping the concept of his/her choices and actions. As an adult and a parent, it is also important that you are able to accept responsibility for your own choices and actions. If you make a mistake, don't be afraid to admit it. Allow yourself to sit down with your child and say "mommy/daddy made a mistake, and I'm sorry, I'll try to do better next time." Also try to give a brief explanation of why the mistake was made. Allow your child to actively communicate their thoughts and feelings back to you. By doing this, you accept responsibility for your own behavior, you develop open communication, and establish trust and honesty with your child. Believe it or not, you also give yourself a break for being human. If you want your child to understand these concepts, you must practice and role model and teach them.

Understanding who you are, what you want for your family and your career is important. If you don't have a sense of direction, you will continue to run in circles, and repeat the same patterns. Everyone wants their child to have *more* or *better* than what they had as a child. But how can you improve on your parenting skills and career goals if you are not honest about where you came from, where you are currently, and where you want to be one, five, or ten years from now. How can you reach these goals of tomorrow if you don't take the steps today?

This is the reason for having you answer the questions about your family dynamics earlier in this chapter. Children who have grown up in these types of family dynamics will likely marry into or carry out the dynamics and patterns into their current family. If there are dynamics that you wish to break the cycle on, then I urge you to consider the following:

- Be honest with yourself
- Identify the concerns or patterns
- Talk with your partner about the dynamics, and discuss setting goals for removing these particular dynamics from your life and your home
- Help each other to grow and gain a better awareness of where you are and where you wish to go
- Identify the steps on how to get there and start putting them into practice
- Identify new and positive goals that are both realistic and obtainable

- Begin to implement these new forms of communication and strategies within your home

I recognize this sounds easier said than done; it will take an effort and commitment on all parties involved. However, the good news is that the cycles or patterns can be broken. To break a habit takes consistent daily effort, and sometimes even a minute to minute effort. You must become consciously aware of your choices and your actions on a daily basis. Just remember, you didn't get this way overnight, and the improvements will not happen overnight. Once again, change begins from within, it begins with you. It takes time, effort, and commitment.

I have included a self-inventory in this chapter. Use the inventory for yourself, your partner, and you might even use parts of it to try to gain a better understanding of your child. This inventory is not a test. There are no right or wrong answers. The answers are yours and yours alone. It's about you and will allow you to gain a concrete perspective of where you are in your life. It will also give you an opportunity to recognize and to expand upon your strengths and weaknesses. I also hope it will help you to identify and set goals for yourself, your family, and your career. You may even complete one with your partner in mind, and have your partner complete with you in mind. Then take the opportunity to compare each other's inventories. This will give you an idea on how you may be perceived by someone else and provide an opportunity on how to make positive changes. Keep in mind while comparing inventories, that effective communication and active listening skills should be implemented. This is a time to listen to constructive criticism and to help each other begin working toward a positive change. It is not a time to become judgmental, defensive, and/or critical. This inventory is designed to help you to take an honest look at yourself, and to give you ideas on how you can make positive changes for yourself. The only way it will be effective is through your own honesty in answering the questions. This inventory is not to be used to beat yourself up. It is to be used as a constructive, positive tool in an effort to help you to improve. We all have strengths and weaknesses. Work to expand upon your strengths and improve them. If you increase the awareness of your strengths and improve upon them, then the weaknesses will lessen.

Self-inventories are not easy. It's not always easy to look in the mirror; however, you need to observe your own situation to be able to make the first step toward self-improvement. Remember this phrase: "no matter where you go, there you are." It's time to stop running from the person that holds the key to change—you! To gain respect, we must earn respect and begin to establish respect for ourselves as a person, A great place to start is by accepting responsibility for our own choices and our own actions. We all want our children to have more than we had, but how can we provide that for them if we don't model that behavior? Once you establish true faith in your own spirituality and within yourself, anything is possible!

Self-Inventory

Self-Inventory
Write down your answers on a separate sheet of paper
Who am I? (Identify at least five positive aspects of yourself)
Where do I see myself as: (A parent; a husband/wife; in my job/career, as a supervisor/employee/colleague) today, and over the next month/six months/one year from now?
What aspects would I like to work on to improve?
How can I set goals and take steps to improve?
Do I accept responsibility for my choices and my actions?
If yes, list three ways I have accepted responsibility in the last six months and over the past year.
If no, why do I not accept responsibility for my choices and actions and behaviors?
What do I gain by not accepting responsibility?
What do I lose by not accepting responsibility?
How do I feel if I am the one who "passes the buck" or blames someone else for my choices and actions?
Who am I helping by not accepting responsibility for my choices and actions?
Who am I hurting by not accepting responsibility for my choices and actions?
If I could change one thing about myself what would it be? Why? And how can I begin to change it?
List three goals and set time frames on how I can begin to make a change on the above question.
Name one quality that I really like/admire about myself
List three ways I can use the above quality to enhance myself and those around me.
List my strengths and weaknesses for each of the following categories:

My Strength as a:	My Weaknesses as a:
Parent to my child/children:	Parent to my child/children:
Husband/Wife to my partner:	Husband/Wife to my partner:
Employee; Supervisor:	Employee; Supervisor:
Co-Worker:	Co-Worker:
Brother/Sister to my own siblings:	Brother/Sister to my own siblings:
A child daughter/son to my own parents:	A child daughter/son to my own parents:
An adult daughter/son to my own parents:	An adult daughter/son to my own parents:

Once you have identified your strengths and weaknesses, list at least one way you can expand upon each of your strengths, and how that may benefit you.

After identifying your weaknesses, list at least one main weakness within each category that you would like to change. Then identify how changing that weakness would benefit you.

After identifying the above information, set obtainable goals and set realistic time frames to enhance your strengths and to improve upon your weaknesses. Then list at least three steps you will need to take to obtain each individual goal.

Do not overwhelm yourself and attempt to change too many things. Set your goals and realistic time-frames in order to start making positive changes.

You can work with your partner and family to help you establish and obtain your goals. They may want to do their own self-inventory and begin making changes also. Be creative and hold scheduled family meetings to update your progress and the progress of your family. Make this an enjoyable and educational assignment, but also be ready to listen and accept constructive criticism when necessary.

Keep in mind that this is not a fast process and it takes commitment and work. You didn't get here overnight and things will not change overnight. Remember that if you set your mind to achieve something that you feel is important, then, anything is possible. Believe in yourself, you can do it!

3 Dealing with Feelings (Including Grief and Loss)

I don't want to take away from the other chapters in this book, but I feel this is one of the most important chapters. In today's society, we pass our co-workers in the hall, and someone will always say, "How are you today?" Our usual answer is "fine" or "okay," and we both keep walking in opposite directions. Now you know the person that asked, "How you were doing?" didn't really care if you were having a horrible day, or if you're having an exceptionally great day. "How are you?" has become something we seem to say in passing. On the other hand, by answering the question "fine" or "okay" seems to be the logical and hurried response to the question. The point I'm making is that we don't take the time to see how someone really does feel, nor do we take the time to inventory our own feelings.

Let's take a moment to slow down and actually identify and define feelings and their counterparts—emotions. Webster's Dictionary (1999), defines feelings as "the condition of being aware; consciousness, what a person feels deeply inside: love, hate, joy, sadness, etc. The way a person is able to react emotionally to someone or something."

Webster's Dictionary (1999), also defines emotions as "any particular feeling, such as love, hate, joy, sadness. Feeling is a less formal word meaning the same thing, but can also suggest a sharing of another's emotion."

By considering these two definitions, we will discuss feelings and emotions and will use them interchangeably throughout this chapter.

If we are unable to inventory our own feelings, then how can we expect our children to become more aware of their feelings? Also, I want to alert you to the fact that the words: *fine, good, bad,* and *okay* are NOT feelings or emotions. Even with new technology and easier ways of doing things, somehow we have lost how to take the time to inventory and express how we feel. I like to say the terms *good, bad, fine,* and *okay* have become our quick and easy *drive through* terms at the feeling's convenience store.

Feelings come in many forms, but most of us use terms such as *fine* and *okay* because those terms have become a quick and easy answer. We don't have to think about what we are saying. But what exactly does *fine* and *okay* mean? Those are such generalized terms that could encompass numerous things and no one really knows what it means for the person verbalizing it. Even the person verbalizing these terms has not really given true thought or meaning to them. Words such as *happy, excited, joyful, sad, frustrated,* and *angry* are true feeling terms that most of us would have to take a minute to consider and recognize before we expressed them.

So why take the time? If we take the time to consider and recognize real feeling terms, then we actually have to assess what we are truly feeling in that particular moment more effectively. For example, if we took a moment to consider, *"I'm getting frustrated,"* could help slow down the momentum that could be leading to actual anger or explosiveness. It also stops us from just blurting out the *drive-through* statement: *"I'm fine."* When you just say, *"I'm fine"* you are not actually thinking or dealing or recognizing how you truly feel. *"I'm fine"* or *"I'm okay"* shuts down any open form of communication. Those statements do not allow you to feel and recognize what is going on within you at that moment. If you take a moment to actually recognize and verbalize a real feeling term, such as *"I'm frustrated"* it not only slows you down to rationally think about your feelings, but leaves the door open to actual communication and awareness of what that feeling means for you and the person you are saying it too. No one really knows what *fine* and *okay* means, but we are aware of the meanings of the words like *happy, excited, sad, frustrated, angry,* etc. By doing this, we can stop or slow down the feeling or outburst of anger that came from the initial feeling of *being* frustrated or overwhelmed.

If you begin to practice identifying your emotions as they arise, and deal with them as they arise, it will take some stress off of you as a person. Ignoring feelings does not make them go away; it only increases your own anxiety and stress level. When you gain an awareness of your own feelings, you are able to deal with your children more effectively. You can now teach your children actual feeling terms and help them to identify their own feelings. You can communicate with them in a more effective manner as well. I tell families that if you have had a bad day at work and have not dealt with your feelings, who do you think is going to catch those pinned up feelings when you walk through the door?

We all have tough days, but the key is identifying feelings as they arise and deal with them instead of suppressing them and breaking down later or hurting someone else's feelings. That will only lead to another feeling: *guilt.*

I have included a "Feelings Face Sheet" to re-educate you on actual feeling terms. I ask parents to use this at home and make a game out of it. Everyone sits down, takes a few minutes to look at the sheet, and identifies some of the feelings that each person experienced that day. Once the feelings are identified, each family member relates what triggered each of those feelings. Not only does the family take a few qualitative minutes out of their day; they create a time of learning, bonding and communicating within the family. It only takes a few minutes and provides quality family time.

Another activity you can use is the *High-low* game. Turn off the television, sit down for dinner and each person in the family reflects upon their day. They discuss the high point of their day and identify feelings associated with the high point. They also reflect upon their low point of the day and discuss the feelings associated with the low point of the day. This helps everyone communicate and listen to each other about how their day really transpired. It not only opens doors for positive, active communication and relationship building but also builds trust and support. You can also play this game with your children and their friends.

Another benefit of the feeling time is that it helps to identify possible problems the child may be having with a peer. The family can help the child with possible alternatives to deal with that peer more appropriately and have a follow-up discussion about how the alternatives worked or didn't work.

This feeling time has also been implemented in the early-childhood educators' guide of *Bridging the Gap* to provide children an opportunity to identify their feelings during the day and help to provide a group discussion among the children. This enhances thought processes and communication skills among the children. It is important that the educator facilitates this process and listens to what the children have to say about themselves and about each other. The educator can take this time to involve the children in brainstorming ideas to help a peer to deal with a specific situation. It also helps children to socialize and think about what they want to say. This is an excellent time to help a shy or reclusive child incorporate peer involvement, and discuss some feelings that he or she may be experiencing.

The other section of this chapter deals with grief and loss. This is important because children's environments change daily. Grief and loss not only surround death, but they can also result from parental separation and divorce. Loss can be identified as an act of losing someone or something that is important to an individual. The feeling of grief is identified after the act of losing someone or something takes place, or during a time of transition, such as a divorce or a major illness.

Grief entails varying emotions such as sadness, anger, guilt, anxiety, and helplessness. During a time of grief and loss, the parent needs to allow the child to process feelings and questions. Communication between the parent and the child, along with the educator and the child's family is very important during this time of transition. The educator can be a great benefit for both the child and the child's family in that the educator is a neutral party and can help the child to process more openly. It is also important that the parent and the educator maintain and monitor contact on how the child is processing and working through the phases of grief and loss.

In helping a child work through the grief and loss process, it is important for the parent and the educator to be supportive and a good listener. The parent and educator need to allow some "one on one" time to process the child's questions and feelings. The educator can also provide a special group time to allow the child and his or her peers discuss feelings, and provide their own supportive feedback to the child. Through all of this, the parent and educator need to keep in mind that grief and loss is a process and that anyone experiencing grief and loss will have both good and bad days. During this time of transition, consistent, regular communication between the family and the educator needs to be maintained.

This chapter also has enclosures for feeling activities to help children identify and communicate their feelings more appropriately. These activities are also enclosed in the *Educator's Guide for Bridging the Gap*. The purpose of this program is to allow everyone to work together. It is also a way to provide communication between families, children, and their educators

Feeling Activities

Below you will find activities and ideas to help you implement the awareness and understanding of feelings within your family. This information is provided to help you as a parent to be creative and implement an awareness of feeling terms within your home. This information may be implemented in short increments of time to enhance quality communication within the home. It is meant to be fun and informative—not a chore. Use these ideas as examples and be creative to enhance them or implement new ones.

The first activity is to identify feelings with the expressions on the feeling faces. This is appropriate to allow the children to identify what they are feeling and what happened to cause them to feel that particular way. The three keys to using this activity are:

1. Identify a feeling using a feeling word.
2. Tell what caused that particular feeling.
3. Explain how they dealt with that feeling.
4. If they were unable to deal with the feeling appropriately, help them to come up with better alternatives to express their feelings appropriately.
5. If they expressed their feelings appropriately, provide praise.

For example, identify the feeling of happy. What made them happy and how did they show happiness. Did it make them laugh, want to play or dance or tell someone? Identify feeling of mad or angry. What made them mad or angry? Did they cry, stomp around, slam a door, etc.? Is there a more appropriate way to handle the anger?

This activity will cause the child to think, communicate and learn more about him/herself. It should also help the child to understand and deal with feelings more appropriately. Anger is a feeling, and it's okay to be angry. It's how a person deals with his or her anger that becomes a problem. The parent can help the child brainstorm ideas on how to handle his or her feelings more appropriately and then begin to help the child to practice and role-play some of those ideas. Role-playing also gives children an opportunity to see for themselves how they may act in certain situations.

Please note: Role playing is not to be used to degrade a child in any way; it is merely a tool to spark education, ideas and interest.

Parents may also use this activity in their home to initiate creativity and conversation. How many times have you asked your child, "What did you do in school today?" How many times have you gotten this response, "Nothing." Many times, after the answer of "nothing" has been stated, we have just run out of what to say or how to obtain new answers or conversation. Use these activities in your home. They are easy to use and provide quality conversation and creative thinking time. It doesn't take a long time to implement them in your home and will provide enhancing conversation with the entire family, and most importantly with your child.

Since time is a factor in all our lives, you can even use this information while cooking supper or driving. You will find that the Feelings Sheet does not encompass all the feelings and emotions that we encounter. Use the sheet as an educational tool for your family. Identify new feelings and allow your child to draw his or her own feeling faces. Once the child has drawn feelings faces, allow a few minutes to process with the child about the feelings and the cause(s) of the feelings.

Exercise #1: Feelings Game: Allow the child to stand up and make a feeling expression on his or her face. Other children can then guess feeling terms that match the child's expression. This game can help the children to see how peers/siblings may perceive them when making certain faces. It also allows them to remain in touch with how their feelings affect their own expressions. I encourage the parent to be active and make his or her own feeling faces for the children to guess feeling terms. It can help the parent to see how the child may perceive them in certain situations. This game may also initiate the ability to more effectively read social cues from others. It may even be used at a social gathering such as the child's birthday party.

Exercise #2: High-Low Game: Discuss the day's events with your child. Ask them the high point of their day and allow them to tell you. Discuss the low point of their day and allow them to discuss it. It may not seem huge or relevant to you as to their highs and lows; however, it is relevant to them. Actively listen and communicate about these events. Provide positive, motivating responses to them. Discuss the high and low of your day. Keep it simple and allow them to provide positive feedback and ideas to you as well.

I am feeling _____

Other feelings:
frustrated, worried, shy, upset

4 Establishing Rapport and Self-Esteem

This chapter is a follow-up to Chapter 2 in understanding who you are as a parent. If you have children, you need to understand your own boundaries and limitations. If you were honest in filling out the self-inventory, then this chapter should enhance what you may have chosen to work on for yourself and your parenting skills.

Remember when you were small and your mother or father stood up over you, possibly pointing their finger at you, and telling you what you should or should not do? By them standing over you and pointing a finger may have been a little intimidating; don't you think? Children will give you more respect if you become more consciously aware of your own body language and verbal tone. If you want a child to respect and communicate with you, then place your physical self on their level and look them in the eye. Don't be afraid to get down on the child's physical level when you are communicating with them. It's no different than if you were trying to make a good impression in an interview.

In an interview, you would make a better impression by internally monitoring your physical stature and looking the interviewer in the eye rather than being all bent over and looking down at the floor. Also, how probable are your chances of getting hired for a job, if you stood over your prospective new boss and pointed your finger at him or her? On the other hand, if you were the prospective interviewer, would you be prone to hire someone who looked you in the eye and openly communicated with you rather than looking to hire someone who mumbled in a very low tone of voice and was always looking away?

As discussed previously, everyone has feelings, and even at an early age, children are gaining a sense of awareness and are establishing their own self-esteem. If a child lives in a home and goes to school or daycare in an environment filled with consistency and positive reinforcement, that child is likely to exhibit healthy skills and positive choices. On the contrary, a child who lives in an environment filled with negativity, anger and inconsistency is more likely to act out to obtain negative reinforcement because that is what has been role modeled for them in their environment.

People seem to categorize children in one of two ways: *good* or *bad*. You've heard the saying that the "squeaky wheel gets the grease." *Good kids* usually receive positive reinforcement, while *bad kids* usually receive negative reinforcement. Either way, the child receives some type of reinforcement. The term reinforcement is interchangeable with attention. Children love attention and want to be positively reinforced or noticed. However, sometimes the only attention a child receives is negatively reinforced. As adults, we want to be recognized for our accomplishments or for what we do. We all want and need to feel that we matter. We look to be reinforced on a positive level by others and to be noticed in a positive way. Our children are the same way. They want to be loved and accepted. They want praise for their actions.

In the category of good and bad, I want to discuss a third category that most of us overlook. The third category is the child, who sits alone and doesn't say anything, or bother anyone. We usually like this child because he or she usually doesn't cause us problems. However, we also seem to overlook this child as we are spending our time dealing with the *good kids* or the *bad kids*. After all, we have to expend our energy on the positive or negative children. Remember that "squeaky wheel" thing. These children know how to seek and get attention, whether it is positive or negatively reinforced. They are the squeaky wheels, and they get the grease.

However, let's refer to the third category as *the falling through the cracks child*. In most cases, I have found that these children usually fall behind because they don't receive any genuine reinforcement—be it positive or negative. They don't expend any energy to learn to act either positive or negative, just as we don't necessarily expend our energy encouraging them to socialize and communicate. Therefore, this child usually develops poor social skills and has low or no self-esteem. This child will retreat inwardly and will fall behind both emotionally and educationally. These children can easily become one of our statistics because as they get older, their self-esteem and sense of identity are not well developed. Often these children fall into the wrong crowd and make poor choices. There are many types of behaviors and personalities; however, for this chapter I am mainly discussing these three types of children: positive attention seekers, negative attention seekers, and those who, for whatever reason, seem to fall through the cracks.

Below are some characteristics of a low self-esteem:

- Inability to accept compliments
- Lack of pride in caring for oneself
- Takes blame easily
- Fear of rejection
- Fear of taking risks
- Feelings of worthlessness and inadequacy
- Degrades him/herself (I'm bad, I'm ugly, I'm a failure, etc.)

- Inability to identify positive aspects about himself or herself
- Difficulty maintaining eye contact and effective communication
- Difficulty in socializing/interacting with others
- Difficulty expressing him or herself
- Outbursts of anger and/or aggressive behavior
- Keeps to himself or herself—isolates, may be termed as a "loner."

As mentioned earlier, a positive rapport is important in working with children. The way you, as the parent, approach and communicate with your child will make a difference in helping establish a relationship and being able to work toward identifying positive and negative reinforcements. Your rapport with your child is extremely important in helping him or her increase their personal self-awareness and self-esteem. For a child to listen and accept the possibility that he or she may actually be a good person, the child must have a rapport and relationship that are trustworthy.

Positive reinforcement for your child is critical in establishing a healthy self-esteem. Behavior is learned, and children are not born with low self-esteem. If you as a parent have a low sense of self-worth or self-esteem, then you may be role modeling that for your child. You must be willing to commit to make a difference in your life. In turn, that will help to improve your relationships with your family. In my book, *The Resume of Life*, I discuss the importance of taking care of yourself and the power of affirmations. Here's an excerpt taken from page 73 that sums it up nicely:

It is never too late to change or make a difference. If you're having thoughts like I'm too old, I'm too fat, or I'm too tired, or I'm too whatever, then start now to change your energy by releasing those negative thoughts and change them to: I can, I will and I am. Begin to believe in you. Do not allow anyone to tell you or to make you feel less than who you really are."

Once you do this for yourself, you can easily role model it for your children.

Below is a list of self-esteem boosters:

- Positive affirmations: begin positive self-talk with the words: *I can; I will* and *I am*. For example, *I am loving; I am happy; I am worthy; I am successful*, etc. Teach and role model positive affirmations to your child. Use positive feeling words and say them numerous times a day. Make it fun, and once you change your thoughts to positive affirmations, you will begin to feel and believe and see the difference in yourself. In turn, you will be much more effective in teaching and role modeling it to your child.
- Reinforce successful behaviors.
- Don't be critical and quick to criticize.
- Don't ignore or overlook successful behaviors or accomplishments.
- Celebrate successful behaviors with joy, praise and encouragement.
- Help your child to express his or her thoughts and feelings.
- Realize that everyone makes mistakes, even as adults. Help your child to learn and grow from mistakes. Do not belittle or degrade them. Talk it through and remain

open and calm. Anger gets you nowhere and only causes the child to shut down in fear.
- When negative events occur, encourage your child to improve and overcome.
- Maintain an open line of communication.

It is also important for you, as a parent, to intervene in your child's life at an early age. It is time to begin to closely monitor the following:

- What your child is reading
- What your child is watching on television
- How your child is interacting online
- What your child is listening to in terms of music
- Who your child is creating peer relationships with

The earlier you intervene and monitor the above, the easier it will be as your child gets older. If you begin this intervention at an early age, the child will learn self-respect as he or she moves into adolescence. This intervention also becomes important in building a trusting bond not easily severed when your child becomes an adolescent. It is easier to help your child establish positive self-worth and understand the difference between right and wrong at an early age rather than waiting and trying to intervene during adolescence.

You may have heard the phrase, "expect the worst and hope for the best." If you build an honest, trusting bond with your child at an early age and establish positive self-esteem, the less likely he or she will have negative problems as an adolescent. In today's society expect that your child will be exposed to negative influences such as alcohol, drugs, sex, and violence. Technology is prevalent in all our lives, and the best offense is a good defense.

- Be actively involved in your child's life.
- Help them to overcome obstacles and continue to build and maintain a trusting, respectful relationship.
- Become consciously aware of your body language and your verbal tone.
- Become a sounding board to encourage your child to communicate with you and not be afraid you will become angry over anything they want to discuss with you. Again, if you instill fear, you will only cause the child to shut down and be afraid to talk to you about what may be going on at school or among their peers.

Expect that eventually your child will be exposed to these negative influences. Educate yourself about them on the front end, and you can keep an open line of communication with your child. In addition, you can hope for the best on the flip side that as they get older, they will know they can come to you with their concerns.

You need to know that your child will be exposed to and may experiment with alcohol, drugs, and sex. However, if you have established communication, and instilled a positive awareness, then hopefully your child will be strong enough to know he or she can come to you for advice and help to avoid these negative influences.

The hope is if your child experiments with alcohol, drugs, and sex that he or she will have a strong sense of self-worth established early on, and other important interests and activities that will help him or her to recognize immediately that alcohol, drugs, and/or sex are not needed to prove anything to anyone. *"Just Say No"* is a concept, and your child cannot be expected to "just say no" if there is no strong sense of identity and self-worth. As the parent, you need to help your child develop a positive sense of self at an early age. As with all things, ignoring a problem or issue will not make it go away. Again, remember to educate yourself and be a positive role model and active participant in your child's life.

I am including some examples of self-esteem exercises within this chapter. Use these exercise to help expand your creativity. Remember to make them relevant, interesting and educational for you and your family.

Self-Esteem Exercises

Exercise #1: The Power of Affirmations: Sit down with your child/children and have each child say something positive about him- or herself. This can include what they like about themselves (eye color, hair, smile, etc.) Next, the parent needs to give positive reinforcement about the child's response. After this process, allow the child to elaborate on reasons why their responses are positive. For example: "I have pretty eyes, or I am kind." (The parent may respond, "What do you think is special about your eyes?" The child responds, "Because they're big and blue.") The parent then responds to this statement with positive reinforcement.

How this helps:

This exercise allows the child to identify something positive about self and provides an opportunity to expand on the initial statement, while receiving positive reinforcement from the adult and initiating thought and conversation.
The parents need to provide positive affirmations about themselves and allow the child to interact and provide reinforcement on what the parent is saying also.

Exercise #2: The parent needs to be actively involved to facilitate this exercise to ensure it remains on a positive, complimentary level. This can be done with siblings, other family members, or even peers who are visiting your home. Allow the children to sit in a circle (including the parent), and have each child make a positive statement about someone in the group. Once child A makes a positive statement about child B, allow child B to accept the compliment from child A, along with discussing how it felt to be given that compliment.

How this helps:

This enhances awareness of positive reinforcement and communication skills.

***Exercise* #3:** Allow the child to discuss something special that has happened that day. How did the event affect the child? What was the child's role in the event? Allow the child to describe the feelings that he or she felt during the event. (Hint: use feeling terms.)
As the parent, becoming an active listener and helping to maintain communication by asking questions, allows the child to show feelings and describe the day's events.

*Use these exercises as a guide to be creative in working with your child. In a matter of a few minutes, you can have a positive, uplifting conversation with your child, and spend quality time allowing your child to trust and bond with you.

5 Coping Skills

When working with children, we need to have an understanding of how we and our children cope with stressful situations. In this chapter, we will consider coping skills and respect.

Coping skills denote how a person or child deals with a particular situation. As a parent, think about your child and ask yourself these questions. How does my child cope with problems at school or at home? How does my child cope with peers and/or other adults?

As an adult and a parent, take a moment to think about how you deal with the following questions. How do I cope with problems at work or at home? How do I cope with other adults/peers/co-workers or my child in stressful situations?

Below are some ways or defense mechanisms that adults and children use to cope with particular situations. We all have coping mechanisms that we use during stressful, fearful or painful situations. After asking yourself the above questions, see if you can identify any of the following coping skills to help you with your answers.

Coping Skills:

- Daydreaming
- Not sleeping or sleeping too much (including lethargy)
- Shutting down
- Keep trying again and again to make something work or fit
- Overeating or refusing to eat
- Isolates

- Fighting or abusive to self
- Denial
- Hyperactivity or overly nervous
- Acting helpless
- Somatic (stomach aches, headaches, physical complaints)
- Excessive crying
- Acting out or anger outbursts
- Blaming
- Drug/Alcohol abuse
- Excessive worry
- Overspending

These are just a few examples of coping skills. I am sure you can think of others. Keep in mind that we all have our own set of coping mechanisms, and we use different ways of coping depending on the situation that we are confronted with at the time. Once you've identified the coping mechanism(s) you or your child uses, ask yourself: Are these coping mechanisms helping or hindering us? My guess is they bring about further feelings of anxiety, shame, fear or guilt.

On the other hand, you should be aware that not all coping skills are negative or designed to bring about further feelings of negativity. However, as with anything, it can be taken to the extreme. Some coping skills that we may consider to be more positive are:

- Exercise
- Meditation
- Discussing feelings and situations
- Writing or drawing
- Relaxation
- Playing with pets

- Taking a "mental health day" off from work
- Talking to or helping others
- Listening to music

Once you have identified your own coping mechanisms, take a moment to compare them with the coping mechanisms that you identified for your child. Are there similarities between the coping mechanisms that you use and those of your child? Likely, you will find similarities, and may want to try to change any negative coping skills into positive coping skills and strategies. However, the work begins with you as the role model.

Again, behavior is learned and you are the one to role model either positive or negative behaviors to your child. You are also the one to identify and role model positive and effective ways to cope with various situations when they arise. Your child watches and learns from you. For example, if your coping mechanism(s) are excessive worry or angry outbursts and your child is aware of this, what do you think your child feels when you respond and act this way? What do you think your child learns from you when you exhibit these types of behaviors?

If you or your child is having difficulty in dealing with others, or dealing with stressful situations and exhibiting poor coping skills, I have added some exercises to give you new ideas and alternatives. Use these scenarios and build upon them to develop new scenarios with your child.

Keep in mind that these skills did not develop overnight, and will not improve overnight. These exercises are only to assist you in helping yourself and your child find new and more creative ways to handle various stressful situations. Once you begin working on this for yourself and then with your child, it is extremely important that you implement these skills on a regular and consistent basis. It takes less time to implement and reinforce positive coping skills, social skills and manners at an early age than it does if you wait and expect the child to begin to learn it later after he or she may have gotten involved in negative activities.

Let's turn our attention to discuss respect and manners. Manners and respect are polite ways of acting or behaving in a particular situation. Some aspects of manners and respect include, but are not limited to the following:

- Not interrupting when someone is talking
- Covering your mouth when sneezing or coughing
- Sincerely apologizing when needed
- Maintaining eye contact when speaking to someone
- Using terms such as Ma'am or Sir
- Saying "please," "thank you," and "excuse me"
- Helping others or holding a door open for others
- Maintaining appropriate hygiene and appearance
- Being kind and respectful of others

Exhibiting manners and respect are actions and phrases that nowadays are taken for granted and forgotten in our fast-paced, changing society. These are simple concepts that will help the child to develop more self-respect and enhance self-esteem in her or her future growth. If you, as an adult, are in a store, and you see a child who has been taught to use appropriate manners and social skills, you will probably respond by smiling and communicating with him or her. You will also witness positive responses from the child's parent or guardian. Most likely that child has been taught to have manners and receives positive reinforcement from the parents. On the other hand, if you witness a child who is acting out, rude, and not listening, you will probably turn and walk away or show some other type of negative response. Likely, you will also hear that child's parent yelling, threatening or demeaning him or her. That child also is likely a product of an environment similar to its behavior. Which child do you think will be more prone to feeling better about himself or herself and more prone to listen and communicate more effectively?

If a child displays acceptable manners, he or she is more likely to be open and receptive to new ideas and concepts in both educational and social settings. As a parent, it is your responsibility to help maintain consistency and role modeling behaviors while educating the child to use proper manners and to establish the ability to give and to gain respect. To gain respect, you must first earn respect. To earn respect, you must first respect yourself and others. This will enhance positive responses for the child both in social settings and at home. It will also contribute to his or her own social skills and self-esteem.

Coping Skills and Activities

Ideas for Coping Skills and Manners

Exercise 1:

One day Johnny was playing with Susie on the playground. While they were playing, Susie asked Johnny if she could play with one of his toys. This toy was very special to him and he told Susie that she could not touch the toy. How should Susie "cope" with Johnny's answer?

(The parent may help the child/children brainstorm numerous answers. The parent may also give some alternative coping skills to allow the children choose a specific answer. For example, should Susie run off and cry, take the toy anyway, get up and yell or refuse to play with Johnny? Could Susie try to talk about why he won't let her play with the toy, or find a different toy to play with? What other things could either Johnny or Susie do? This will allow for discussion of why the child/children chose a specific answer and brainstorm possible solutions to handle being told "no" in a more appropriate manner.

Part 2: Johnny allowed Susie to play with the toy, however, Susie took the toy and broke it on purpose. How will Johnny feel? How will Johnny respond? Why did Susie break the toy? What could make this situation better for both Johnny and Susie?

Part 3: Johnny allowed Susie to play with the toy and they began to talk and play together. How does Johnny feel? How does Susie feel? Did they have a good time and share with each other? Did they show respect and manners toward one another?

(There are numerous ways to act out the responses for Johnny and Susie. As a parent, help your child to find the best solutions for the scenarios. Be creative and help to educate them about positive coping skills, respect, and manners.)

Exercise 2:

One day Sharon was sitting in the classroom and the teacher asked Sharon if she would draw a picture on the board. Everyone in the class turned to see if Sharon would go to the board to draw the picture, but Sharon did not get up. (Could Sharon have been daydreaming? Did she give up without trying? Was she afraid to go to the board?, etc.) What types of coping skills was Sharon using? Why did Sharon not respond to the teacher's request to go to the board to draw the picture? What could the teacher do to help Sharon? How could Sharon's peers help and support her? What types of manners or positive responses from her peers could be acceptable to help support Sharon? What are some positive coping skills that might help Sharon?

**Be creative with these scenarios with different responses and different outcomes. Allow your child to be creative and come up with new scenarios and outcomes by using negative coping skills vs. positive coping skills and how each one feels in the scenario. Work with your child and allow him/her to come up with an event that may have happened at school and what the outcome was and how the outcome could have been better if....?

This will enhance rapport and communication between you and your child. It will also allow the child to think and learn how to respond appropriately when certain negative situations arise.)

6 Communication and Listening Skills

Throughout this program, we have touched on various skills involving communication. I feel that we need to take it a step further, and actually discuss the importance of communication. After all, communication is the way we relate to one another.

We express ourselves in different ways to communicate with one another. We can communicate through both verbal and nonverbal behaviors. Verbal communication is comprised of verbally speaking to someone and having a conversation. Nonverbal communication is comprised of our actions and body language. In working with children, we need to remember that our actions and tone of voice speaks louder than words.

As adults, we are obviously physically taller than our children, and if we always stand over them while communicating with them, they can be somewhat overwhelmed. To help a child to be more productive and to learn, we need to always be aware of what our body language is expressing.

If a child needs discipline, standing over him or her could be more effective. If a child needs positive interaction or reinforcement, placing yourself at that child's eye level may be more effective. To place yourself at that child's eye level may involve bending or squatting down or even picking the child up. Below are some forms of nonverbal communication to help you assess how you may be approaching your child during the communication process:

- Open body posture: uncrossed legs and arms, open hands, eye contact, positive facial expressions

- Defensive body posture: clenched fists, turning away, crossed legs or arms, limited or no eye contact, staring with an angry expression, wringing hands, finger pointing, angry stance with hands on hips
- Cooperative body posture: leaning forward, sitting on edge of the chair, speaking openly, eye contact, smiling, positive facial expressions

Becoming consciously aware of your nonverbal communication, tone of voice, and thinking about what you are going to verbalize will make a huge difference in how the child perceives you. This will also affect how the child will respond to what you are saying. Taking a moment to assess your posture, along with thinking about what you are going to say and the tone of voice you use will provide you with more success and validity in getting your point across.

For example, Joey is running around the room and will not listen to the adult who asks him to sit with the rest of the children. The adult is standing on the other side of the room and screaming at him in a loud voice, "SIT DOWN and SHUT UP!"

- Can you identify nonverbal and verbal communication in this scenario?
- Can you identify preferable alternatives and solutions?
- How do you think this action and tone of voice affected Joey?
- How might he have responded to the adult?
- Could this cause some self-esteem concerns for Joey or even the children that witnessed this event?
- What did the other children experience from witnessing this scenario and watching and listening to the adult?

- If the adult had gone over to the child and placed him- or herself at eye level, and spoken directly to Joey, would that have made a difference?
- Could it have made a difference with the other children in the room?
- If the adult was consciously aware of his or her nonverbal communication and tone of voice, would that have made a difference?

At the end of this chapter, I will provide information for different types of communication and awareness of obstacles to effective communication.

Active listening is the other form of communication. One of the most effective ways to gain knowledge and awareness is the art of active listening. We all like to be heard and to have the opportunity to express what we want to say. However, we have a tendency to take others for granted or second-guess what the person is saying because we are not actively listening to them. Oftentimes we are focused on other things while they are speaking to us. We don't take that moment to actually hear or focus on what someone is saying to us. When we do this, we are not really listening or grasping the actual concept of what someone is telling us. The point I am making is that we are all human, and we all have times when we do not actively listen.

The art of active listening is especially difficult for children to comprehend, and this can cause great frustration to adults. On the other hand, as adults, do we take the time to actively listen to what our children are trying to tell us? I use the term "art of active listening," because it is an art. It is something you practice and become consciously aware that you do to hear what is being said. It is a time when you actually stop whatever you are doing and take that moment to focus on the other person and what they are saying. It is a time when you actually listen and engage with an appropriate response.

When communicating with a young child, keep in mind that they comprehend in literal, concrete terms. Think back to my example in chapter one regarding making a statement that "the grass is not always greener on the other side of the fence." Your child thinks in terms of grass and fences and wonders what color the grass is. So when you talk with your child, give him or her a chance to respond to the point you are expressing to reduce confusion. Allow them to tell you or repeat what they heard you say. This takes effective communication along with both you and the child actively learning and listening to each other.

I am also providing information on various ways to help improve active listening skills at the end of this chapter.

Keep in mind while using this information, to be effective, you need to be consciously aware of both your verbal and nonverbal communication skills. You also need to be consciously aware of the importance of being an active listener. You are the role model and need to enhance your self-awareness in these skills to be effective in helping others. Keep in mind what may seem insignificant to an adult could be enormous to a child. Also, do not forget to praise a child for his or her efforts. Praise is an extremely important tool in developing positive behavior and open communication.

Becoming more consciously aware of your communication skills, both verbal and nonverbal, along with practicing being a more active listener will enhance the relationship between you and your child. It will also help role model and teach your child to do the same. In turn, it will help to increase their socialization skills with others. It should also enhance your other relationships such as your spouse, partner, colleagues, friends, etc. This information is not time consuming, it only requires active and conscious awareness of self. It will increase your chances of getting your point across in a more effective and efficient way.

In discussing effective communication and active listening skills, I would be remiss if I didn't discuss technology. We have entered an age of cell phones, texting, email and social media. Because of the convenience of this technology, we have begun to move away from effective communication. We send a text rather than dialing the phone and having an actual conversation. We send an email at work rather than picking up the phone and having an actual conversation. We get on social media sites and post our thoughts or respond to others with a "like" or a "comment" rather than having an actual conversation. This provides us with convenience and quickness all by a few clicks of a button. If we don't actually feel like talking to someone, we use technology as a way of life and communication for us.

I'm not saying there is anything wrong with this type of technology; however, we seem to have gotten so wrapped up in the ease of it that we have gotten lazy using our communication skills. By doing this, we don't have to look anyone in the eye and have an actual conversation. We don't have to worry about our nonverbal communication nor do we have to actively listen to what someone else is saying to us.

The other issue with this form of technological communication is we can misinterpret an email or text or comment and take it the wrong way. This leads to *mis*-communication, hurt feelings, arguments, etc. Why? Because we can't hear the tone of voice or see the nonverbal communication skills. We are also not actively involved in a back and forth effective conversation of communication and listening.

We are raising our children with this type of convenience and technology and they too are following our lead. If we do not get back to actively communicating and listening, then how can we expect them to learn it? Again, we are the role models, and if we don't teach them effective communication and listening skills, then who will?

Obstacles to Communication

1. Probing for answers:

   - *Who? What? Why? And How?*

     o The adult may not receive answers from the child
     o The child may not understand the point of the question
     o May cause fear and anxiety

   - If the adult chooses to use probing questions, he or she should be aware of nonverbal communication and how the question is stated

   - Be clear about what you are asking. Don't assume the child knows what you want

2. Demanding and demeaning:

   - *You will do this, You must complete this, You have to...*

     o This may result in resistance, retaliation, judging, fear, blaming and/or shutting down

   - *You are a bad kid, You are so lazy, You don't know what you're doing, You were an accident, You act just like...*

     o Child feels demoralized and defeated

- Self-esteem declines
- Communication and listening skills decline
- Retaliation, anxiety, fear, anger
- Shuts down
- Feelings of worthlessness

- Increases possibility of retaliation and begins to judge, blame and/or become aggressive

3. Threatening:

- *You better...If you don't to this, then I'll...You'll do it, or I'll...Do as I say, not as I do...*

    - Produces fear
    - Opens the door to anger, resentment, and/or retaliation
    - Diminishes self-esteem
    - Communication and listening skills decline
    - Child begins to have a "why try" or "why bother" attitude
    - Feelings of worthlessness

Praise and Rewards

We all like to be rewarded for our efforts and as we know, children thrive on extra attention, praise, and rewards.

When providing praise and rewards, keep the following in mind:
- Open nonverbal communication:
    - Face the child
    - Establish eye contact
    - Smile
    - Placing your hand on the child's shoulder, shaking the child's hand, giving a hug, or giving a "high five" (some form of positive physical contact)
- Open verbal communication:
    - Positive, light, enthusiastic tone of voice
    - Stating a clear and positive message
    - Provide uplifting and positive reinforcement as quickly as possible
- Active Listening:
    - Allow the child to physically and/or verbally respond to the praise
    - Allow the child's siblings, peers, or other adults to reinforce the praise
    - Actively listen to and respond to what the child is saying
    - Allow the child to repeat what they heard you say and make sure they understand what you are trying to convey
    - You can repeat to the child what they said and make sure you understand what they are trying to convey

Focus on the child when he or she is speaking and respond accordingly. Oftentimes, we are in such a hurry to fix dinner, etc. we don't take a moment to stop what we are doing and look at the child and actively listen to them.

7 Warning Signs of Abuse and Bullying

This chapter deals with signs of abuse and bullying. It is merely an educational chapter to help the parent to understand the different types of abuse and the signs that accompany various types of abuse issues. These signs and symptoms of abuse do not pose a 100% guarantee that abuse may be occurring, rather they serve as an effort to educate you on what to look for. Bullying and extreme acts of violence have become more prominent in our school systems over the past few years; as parents, we must educate ourselves and become more observant of our surroundings and teach and role model positive behaviors for our children.

There are basically three types of abuse: emotional, physical and sexual. The most difficult type of abuse to prove is emotional. This is because we cannot necessarily physically see or touch it. Emotional abuse consists of constant words that diminish and degrade or belittle a person. Emotional abuse diminishes a person's self-esteem and self-worth. Emotional abuse may also consist of the abuser being easily angered and yelling at the person being abused.

Some signs and symptoms that emotional abuse may be occurring may consist of the following:

- A person exhibits negative self-talk and exhibits feelings of worthlessness
- Low self-esteem
- Somatic complaints: headaches, stomach aches, etc.
- Easily angered and/or hostile/aggressive behaviors
- May degrade and belittle others

- Fantasizes more than the average child
- Anxiety, nervousness, fear
- Impulsive
- School or educational problems (dropping grades, skipping class, etc.)
- When playing with toys such as stuffed animals or dolls, the child may verbalize derogatory statements or anger toward the toy
- Quiet and withdrawn
- Restless and agitated behaviors

If a child exhibits the above behaviors, the parent should monitor and work with the child to allow a more appropriate expression of feelings. The parent should also be aware of his or her communication and listening skills, and allow the child to discuss his or her anger, fear, frustration and various other feelings in a safe and trusting environment.

Unlike emotional abuse, physical abuse is probably the easiest to define because we can actually see and touch it. If a child is being physically abused we can usually see the identifying marks. Physical abuse is not to be confused with the typical bumps and bruises of just being a child.

A person who may be experiencing actual physical abuse may exhibit some of the following:

- Low self-esteem and self-worth
- Exhibits lack of control or is easily angered and frustrated
- Aggressive behaviors
- Impulsive
- Withdrawn
- Likes to hurt or bully other people and/or animals

- Destructive with toys or other people's belongings
- Self-abusive (may hit/cut on self; bang head against a wall, etc.)
- Will have identifying physical marks such as burns and/or bruises that may resemble fingers or punches, cuts and scarring, and/or broken bones
- Impulsive and reckless behaviors
- Declining grades and educational problems
- The child tells stories that do not coincide with the actual physical marks
- Difficulty concentrating and staying on task which can lead to educational problems

If a child exhibits the above behaviors, the parent should attempt to remain as calm as possible while allowing the child a safe place to communicate feelings. The parent should not exhibit extreme anger at this time of disclosure since that may alarm the child further or cause the child to feel as though the abuse is his or her fault. After the disclosure of abuse, the parent should contact the local authorities and report the alleged abuse. With physical abuse, be assured the child has endured emotional abuse as well.

The third type of abuse is sexual abuse. This type of abuse is extremely hard to prove. No one wants to believe that this type of abuse occurs, but the fact remains that it does happen. We need to educate ourselves that sexual abuse is widespread and occurs just as does emotional and physical abuse. Below is a list of behaviors that a child may exhibit if he or she has been sexually abused:

- Breaking rules, fighting and aggression
- Fire setting or preoccupation with fire
- Moody or throwing tantrums, easily angered

- Overeating
- Aggressive
- Impulsive
- Low self-esteem
- Withdrawn
- Sexual acting out and/or displaying inappropriate sexual behaviors
- Running away
- Self-harm and abusive
- Withdrawn and isolating
- Difficulty sleeping and/or nightmares
- Blocking out memories
- School and educational problems (difficulty concentrating, declining grades)
- Poor hygiene
- Possible refusal to use the bathroom and/or soils clothes

If a child exhibits a combination of the above behaviors, the parent should allow the child to open up to the parent in a safe environment and help the child to understand that the abuse was not the child's fault. The parent should contact and report the incident to the local authorities. In any type of abuse, the parent should consider the importance of counseling for the child and the family.

The most important thing to remember is to allow the child to talk about his/her feelings and help the child to understand that the abuse was not his/her fault. Many victims of abuse have feelings of extreme guilt, and feel that they could have stopped the abuse or feel they caused or deserved the abuse. When in fact, most abusers threaten further harm to the child, blame the child for the abuse, or threaten to harm family members if the child tells. It is also important to keep in mind that if any type of abuse is occurring, a large portion of the time the abuser is someone that the family knows.

While the warning signs of abuse do not constitute a 100% guarantee that abuse is occurring, it is important to recognize the common themes in the three types of abuse.

COMMON THEMES:

- Low self-esteem and self-worth
- Easily angered or hostile
- Quiet and withdrawn
- Impulsive
- Restless and/or agitated
- Exhibits self-harm and abusive behaviors
- Difficulty concentrating, educational problems
- Fighting and/or destructive towards people and/or things
- Declining participation in activities that he or she once enjoyed

While discussing abuse, I need to add two more to the list: Bullying and Cyberbullying. Both Bullying and Cyberbullying are the "new" ways for peers to emotionally, physically and even sexually abuse another. Bullying can come in different forms, but in essence, it is abuse. The term "bully" is nothing more than an egotistical word that many feel empowered by and are proud to be called or labeled. However, "bully" is just another name for an abuser. From here on, the term bully and abuser will be used interchangeably as they are one in the same.

Types of bullying can be categorized as the following:

- Verbal Bullying: name calling, offensive and cruel remarks, harassment, threats
- Physical Bullying: Aggression, anger, hitting, fighting, shoving, etc.
- Indirect Bullying: spreading rumors, back stabbing, degrading, intimidation, alienation from groups
- Cyberbullying: The various types of bullying done over social media in the form of personal smears of a person's reputation, hurtful pictures, and spreading rumors by sending out to many people at one time or by threats directly aimed at the victim.

Some warning signs of a child being bullied are:

- Low or decreased self-esteem
- Avoidance of social events or gatherings
- Withdrawn
- Declining grades/problems at school
- Changes in eating and/or sleeping habits
- Anxiety, nervousness, fearful
- Sadness, depression, withdrawn
- Injuries
- Missing or stolen or damaged personal belongings
- Somatic complaints such as headaches, stomach aches, not feeling well
- Changes in activities and/or friends

As you can see, Bullying and Cyberbullying share some of the same signs, symptoms and characteristics to those of emotional, physical and sexual abuse mentioned earlier.

In any type of abuse, there is an abuser/bully and a victim. The bully is in essence an abuser who is abusing another person. The person being abused is the intended target or the victim. It is important to note that abusers/bullies were likely once victims themselves of either abuse and/or bullying.

Some signs of abusive behaviors by an abuser/bully may include:

- Easily angered and argumentative and threatening
- Aggressive and/or violent and destructive behaviors
- Manipulative and judgmental
- Makes false accusations
- Causes others to isolate themselves from their friends and family because of demanding or controlling and/or manipulative behaviors
- Forceful/demanding/jealousy and/or controlling
- Places blame on others for their behavior and actions— "you caused me to get angry and violent because..."
- Targets people they feel are "less than," weak or unworthy
- Unwilling to accept responsibility for own behaviors and actions
- Unrealistic expectations of others—"you must do this or I will..." "If you love me, you will..." "I was violent because I love you and ..."
- Uses the word "love" as a weapon or to control another
- Cruelty to animals and/or children
- Explosiveness and mood swings

When I was in the therapeutic field, we would correlate abusers and victims to that of a pendulum on a grandfather clock. As you know, the pendulum on a clock swings back and forth from one side to the other. Victims and abusers can also do the same. Some victims remain in the victim role and seem to continue to set themselves up in further abusive situations by falling into abusive relationships, etc.

Others may swing from one side to the other: from victim to abuser/bully. In essence, victims can swing to the other side and become abusers/bullies themselves. Both abusers and victims can vacillate from one extreme to the other. If you were able to stop the pendulum on the clock and allow it to come to rest in the middle, that would be where one would find balance and peace and avoid the extremes. I discuss balance and avoiding extremes in my book, *The Resume of Life*.

However, it is very difficult for many victims or abusers/bullies to actually stop and find their balance and their peace because of the trauma and chaos in their life. Instead, they seem to stay in perpetual motion of swinging to the extremes and continue to do harm to themselves and/or to others. This is why it is extremely important for you, the parent, to find your balance and to operate within it so you can role model and teach it to your children and those around you.

I would like to interject a quote from *The Resume of Life* in discussing balance (page 98 – 99):

> *"The only one who can find your balance is you. The only one who can remove yourself from your balance is you. No one did it to you; you allowed it to happen. When you allow people or events to take you out of your balance, you have given them your power and your strength. It is your responsibility to remain in your balance, and to operate within it. If you feel you are being pulled out of balance, then it is your responsibility to recognize it and go back to it. Remember, when your energy is centered in your core—your balance—this is when you are the strongest and most powerful. This is a difficult lesson and thing to do, but*

it can be done and you can do it. Like the pendulum on the grandfather clock, you must be centered to remain restful, peaceful and balanced."

The unfortunate part of this is that these abusers/bullies were once children themselves and likely grew up in some type of abusive environment. They were taught this behavior as a way of life because they grew up in extremes. They have no concept of balance. The more unfortunate part of this today is that our children are getting caught in the cross fire and being exposed to this type of aggression/abuse/bullying more and more. This is why you must work to educate yourself so you can help your children, protect your children and role model positive behaviors, self-esteem, manners, communication skills and respect and balance for yourself and your children. Again, I ask you, if we don't do it....who will? We accepted the role to be a parent and with that role came the responsibility of educating, role modeling and teaching our kids positive ways of being and to become loving and accepting of themselves and others. Our role is not to preach or role model negativity, anger and judgment on ways to harm, hurt, bully or abuse others because of what they have, who they are, or how they look. Our role is to role model positive, accepting, kind, loving and respectful ways to treat ourselves and others.

Victims and abusers/bullies come in all shapes, colors, ages, and sizes. No one is immune to being victimized. However, I do want to provide awareness and education for you in regards to children who may be at greater risk of being abused/bullied and what you can do to help.

1. LGBT Youth: Lesbian, gay, bisexual, or transgender youth and anyone "perceived" as LGBT arc at an increased risk of being bullied or abused.

2. Children with Disabilities: physical, developmental, emotional, intellectual and sensory disabilities are at increased risk of being bullied or abused.
3. Children with Special Health Needs: such as epileptic, severe food allergies, asthmatic, etc. Children who may appear "normal" yet have to be monitored closely for health reasons or take medication.
4. Anyone perceived as being different: overweight, underweight, glasses, how they dress, low income-"perceived" as poor, high income-"perceived" as rich and spoiled, perceived as weak, popularity-doesn't fit in to a "click" or a "group," low socialization skills, quiet, aloof.

Education, acceptance and awareness are keys to helping your children become aware of bullying and abuse. No one, no matter who they are—the color of their skin, their gender, their financial status, their weight, their disability, their appearance, who they love, etc.—should be abused or bullied. No one has the right to judge, demean, degrade or harm another person because of their appearance, skin color, identity, residence, or personal lifestyle.

What you can do:

1. Become a positive and accepting role model for you and your family
2. Educate yourself, role model and teach respect and acceptance to your children
3. Create and provide a safe and trusting environment for your children and their peers
4. If your children are exposed to others with disabilities, or who "seem different," etc., educate yourself about the specific disability or difference and help

your child learn and gain a better understanding of it as well. *Remember, just because someone seems "different" does not give us the right to harm them in any way: emotionally, physically, sexually or by any type of bullying.*
5. Communicate with your child's teachers and stay involved in their activities.
6. Help your children to understand if they witness this type of behavior, it's okay and safe to come to you or to tell someone who can help.
7. Don't be afraid to get involved and to help someone who is experiencing abuse. If your child was a victim of abuse/bullying and someone else knew, would you want them to tell and to help your child or would you rather them turn away and pretend it didn't happen?
8. Form an alliance against bullying with teachers and other parents.
9. Become and remain actively involved in your child's life and education.

8 Parent and Educator Involvement

As you read this chapter, you will find it is directed toward educators and parents to work together and establish consistent communication for the benefit of the child. If your child's daycare or school is using *Bridging the Gap*, this particular chapter should be provided to them. I'm leaving this chapter the same in both the Parent's Guide and the Educator's Guide to provide consistency in the program and establish the importance of the educator and parent working together. Both parents and educators need to be consciously aware of the importance of consistency and working together for the common goal of helping the child to learn and to grow.

One of the most important aspects in working with children is involving the family. My grandfather used to tell me that "the right hand needs to know what the left hand is doing. " To be effective in working with children, educators and parents need to be aware of what is happening or going on with their child each day. If the educators do not inform parents that the child is doing well or that the child may be having difficulty dealing with others or difficulty in obtaining necessary skills, then how can anyone be effective in working with the child? Consistency is the key!

Conversely, if the parent does not take an interest or an active role in their child's life, you can bet that the child will not be effective in informing the parent about his/her day. Do you remember this question, "What did you learn (or do) in school today?" The usual response was, "Nothing." This type of closed-ended question usually receives a one-word answer. Try asking a more open-ended question such as: "Tell me about the best part of your day? Or "Tell me something about your day that you would like to change or improve." These types of questions allow for creativity and fun. The child has to come up with positive aspects of his or her day, and once discussion begins, you may find yourself privy to all kinds of things. At that point, it is very important that you remain engaged, become an active listener, and allow your child to open up. It is extremely important that educators work with parents to maintain consistency in helping a child to learn and grow both emotionally and educationally. The goal is to enhance consistency and communication not confusion.

If a child is doing well in your classroom, don't be afraid to tell the parents. You can talk to the parents in front of the child about how well the child is doing. This will enhance consistency between what the child is working on in your class along with giving that child extra praises in front of the family. Everyone loves to hear good things about themselves and parents love to hear good things about their child. This provides positive reinforcement and enhances self-esteem for the child. During this brief meeting you are able to inform the parent(s) on what skills you are working on in school, (for example, manners and social skills), and reinforce praise to the child. You have also established consistency by allowing the family an opportunity to praise the child and the opportunity to follow up with communication and with the assignment you may be working on.

This meeting has also given the parent(s) an opportunity to talk with the child about what he or she is doing in school. The old, usual answer of "nothing" has now turned into "something" to follow up on and to discuss. So in essence you have provided the parents an opportunity to follow up with the skills you are working on each day with their child which in turn provides consistency. Remember to keep in mind that everyone likes positive attention and praise, and parents love to hear that their child is doing well. You should receive a positive response from the family and know that the family may follow up with more communication and positive reinforcement with the child after they get in the car to leave the school.

On the other hand, you will also have a child who may not be doing so well. It is just as important, if not more so, to discuss these issues with the parents. Don't wait until the child has fallen so far behind that it becomes more difficult to catch up and make improvements. This is the time to pull the parents aside, inform them what you are working on in school, and allow them to provide more communication and consistency for their child. Educators and parents need to work together to help the child. It is extremely important to establish follow up appointments and set goals for the parents and the child in an effort to help the child to grow and to improve. You may even send notes back and forth in an effort to keep both of you informed so the right hand and the left hand can work together to benefit the child.

Most parents want their child to be healthy, happy, and to receive an education. If you establish a positive rapport with the family and set goals, you will likely obtain a positive response and consistent help from them. During this time, positive reinforcement should be given to the child from both the educator and the parents when he or she begins to show improvement.

When the child begins to show improvement, praise should be given immediately along with praising the child in front of the family when they come to pick up the child. Don't stop there but continue to set consistent goals and work with the family. Once you get the ball rolling and improvement is happening, don't drop the ball. Both you and the family must continue to work together in maintaining consistency for the child to continue to grow and show improvement. We are here to teach our children and to even learn from our children. Communication is the most effective key in establishing consistency and helping the child to learn and to grow. If we cannot communicate effectively with one another, how do we propose to help the child to learn effective forms of communication and establish self-confidence and self-esteem?

I am enclosing some sample contracts for parents and educators based on topics discussed throughout the book. Use them as a creative tool and work together to *Bridge the Gap*. The goal is to enhance the child's emotional needs based on feelings, self-esteem, socialization, communication and any other segments of this book that the child may need education and help with in their daily skills and activities. This is a learning process and one that should be consistent during his/her school day along with continued support and consistency at home.

Family Contract and Goals: Feelings

We are currently working on identifying feeling terms and identification of triggers and events that lead to particular feelings. Please help us to follow up with identifying feelings and their triggers while spending time with your child. We are enclosing a feelings face sheet to help work on feelings with your child.

Name:	Date:
Individual Goals:	
Child's Response:	

Thank you,

Family Contract and Goals: Self-Esteem

We are currently working with your child on enhancing his/her self-esteem. Below you will find goals and responses on how your child is doing. Please help us to maintain consistency with your child while working on self-esteem.

Name:	Date:
Individual Goals:	
Child's Response:	

Thank you,

Family Contract and Goals: Socialization Skills

We are currently working with your child to enhance his/her socialization skills. Below you will find information on how your child is progressing on the socialization skills exercises. Please help us to maintain consistency by working with your child on the following goals.

Name:	Date:
Individual Goals:	
Child's Response:	

Thank you,

Family Contract and Goals: Communication and Listening Skills

We are currently working with your child on appropriate communication and listening skills. Please help us to maintain consistency in working on these exercises with your child. Below you will find individual goals and how your child is responding.

Name:	Date:
Individual Goals:	
Child's Response:	

Thank you,

9 Love and Respect vs. Obey and Control

Throughout this book, I have discussed communication and listening skills, feelings, and social skills. I also had you take a self-inventory; hopefully, you have recognized some things that you like about yourself and maybe even noticed some things you may need to work on. This book is to help educate and motivate you to gain a better awareness of who you are and help you to establish change within yourself. If you are able to establish positive change within yourself, then you will gain respect for yourself, provide respect for others, and earn respect from others. Love comes from within and it is up to you to exhibit love and respect to your family and in your outside relationships. You also need to learn to receive love and respect from your family and outside relationships. This is where true change begins. As I mentioned earlier, if you begin to gain a positive awareness of who you are, anything is possible! This will only enhance you, your family, your friends and your relationship with your child.

I have taken theories and psychiatric jargon out of this book and written it in terms that everyone can understand and apply within their own home. This book is to motivate you to be a better person and parent within your own family. It provides you with information to enhance the tools you already possess. The tools you possess within you are the intrinsic desire to be a better person, a better parent, a better friend/colleague and to work with your children and family more effectively. It also makes you aware of the importance of consistency and communication between you and your child's educator. This book does not tell you how you should or should not raise your child; there are enough of those already.

Over the years in working with children and families, the primary common theme is that everyone is different and responds to things differently. This is why I do not believe there is an exact right or wrong way of being a parent. The only thing I can do is to empower you in gaining an awareness of who you are, to become a more effective role model and teacher for your children, and to work with them through respect, love, and communication. These basic keys are something we have gotten away from in this fast-paced society. We have so much technology, and we work so hard just to have a home and pay our bills that we have moved away from basic skills and communication. We have become "driven" and possibly angry within our homes because of the stress we have put ourselves under. Raising a child does not have to be rocket science. It begins with truth, love and acceptance. These are things we all want and need in our life. These are things we all possess, however, we have allowed so many other "things" to get in the way and take our focus off of what is true. We need to find love, peace, balance and acceptance within ourselves and in turn provide it within our homes. We need to get back to the awareness of the importance of family. We seem to have gotten our priorities confused and placed our priorities on "things" and "stuff" and not on family. We've somehow moved away from the "people/human factor" and gotten caught up in money, technology and things that do not have feelings and cannot love us back.

It is extremely important to provide consistency and quality time for your child. It is important to look at your behaviors and how your child perceives you. Also, it is extremely important to communicate and listen to your child. It is time that we stop blaming others or situations and start accepting and role-modeling responsibility for our children and ourselves. This will enhance communication, love and respect in your home. Once you establish this for yourself, then you can easily teach and role model it for your child.

As you see from the above information, the terms *obey* and *control* were not mentioned. That is because you teach your pets to "obey" and they may need to be "controlled." I do not believe obey and control are terms or situations to be placed on children or others. In fact you cannot control another. Keep in mind that if you use control, this may decrease the creativity within your child and could cause him/her to retaliate later. Children need to be worked with and taught in terms of their growth and understanding, not controlled or made to obey commands. The use of respect and responsibility for our actions is much more influential in obtaining positive responses from others. If you have respect in your home, then your child should learn to respect you and listen to what you have to say in terms of discipline. That doesn't mean the child will always be happy or easily accept being disciplined, but he or she should know when mom/dad means business. In no way does this have to come in the form of the parents screaming and throwing their own tantrums. Again, behavior is learned, so what are you teaching?

When I was a young child, I was spending the day with my grandparents who lived across the lake. My mother began calling me to come home for dinner and I did not want to go. My grandfather stated that he was my mother's father and in charge of her and that I could stay with him and not have to go. My mother ended up coming to get me, and by then she was quite upset. I hid behind my grandfather thinking he was the boss and after all, he was her father.

My mother looked at him and stated, "I'm her mother and she needs to listen to me." My grandfather stepped aside and there I stood wide open and nowhere to hide. I learned that day who was in charge. Consistency was implemented and I was unable to use my grandfather's position against my mother to get my way. My grandfather did not interfere with the respect that I should have shown my mother by listening to her.

The next point in this chapter that I want to discuss is consistency and manipulation. When we were children, most of us would ask our mom or dad if we could go somewhere or do something. If we asked mom, and she said "no" (a word none of us like to hear), then we may go ask dad the same question hoping he would say "yes." If dad said "yes," then we successfully manipulated the system. Children seem to learn this skill at an early age, so beware. If you communicate with your family and children effectively, you can minimize this process.

As a child, if I wanted to go somewhere, I would assess which parent I needed to ask to receive a "yes" answer. If I received a "no" from the parent whom I chose to ask, then I would approach the other parent by stating, "Mom said she didn't mind me going, if it's okay with you." At that point, I would usually get an "okay" and then return to mom who originally said "no" and tell her that dad said, "I could do it." By now I have successfully manipulated the situation, not to mention caused them to probably get in an argument. However, I had gotten a "yes" to whatever I planned to do and was on my way. If there had been consistent communication between my parents, my manipulative tactics would have been stopped immediately. Had they communicated and taken the time to make a definitive answer, I would not have been allowed to manipulate them. This also happens frequently in divorced families. You and your ex took on the role of parent and made the choice to have children. No matter what your differences are now, you still need to find a way to communicate effectively when it comes to parenting the child. Do not use your anger and hostility toward each other to hold your child hostage or to manipulate each other. Just as a child learns to manipulate the system, you too are doing the same thing if you are allowing your differences to affect how you are raising the child. Again, I remind you that behavior is learned so what are you role modeling and teaching your child?

The point is that children will manipulate and it is important that you as the parent(s) stay one step ahead of the game. To stay ahead, you need to communicate with your partner and make consistent decisions together. Don't let the child be the "go- between" for you and your partner. Take a moment before giving the child the "go- ahead" to actually talk with your partner about your decision. It will minimize stress, confusion and arguments in the long run. It takes less time to be consistent and communicate with your partner, than if your child manipulates the two of you and you both end up arguing. By communicating with your partner before giving the child your decision also allows you to role model to your child the respect you and your partner have for each other.

In this chapter, as in previous chapters, you will notice that I refer to you and your "partner." I use the term partner because I want you to realize that if you are married or live with someone who is taking an active role in raising your child, the importance of providing consistent partnering and decision making in terms of establishing effective communication, respect and rapport. By doing this, you are role modeling and teaching appropriate behaviors in respect, communication and socialization skills.

If you are divorced, and your ex-spouse has the kids during a specified time, it is even more important that the two of you put your differences aside and attempt to establish as much consistency on decision making as possible. Your child's emotional future depends on it. If there is anger and resentment between you and the child's other parent, it will be much easier for the child to manipulate and retaliate against both you and the other parent. This is the time for you and the other parent to put your personal anger and differences aside, and try to establish some common ground for the child's sake. Please do not use your child as a pawn or a "go between" to enhance your anger toward one another. There was a time the two of you had enough in common to have this child. It is imperative that you maintain some common ground to raise this child. This is not the time to expose your child to your anger and hurt toward your ex-spouse. If you expose your child to your anger and use your child as a "go between," you will eventually lose any respect that child has for you and/or your ex. After all, your child's future and emotional well-being is at risk.

If you are a single parent, it is important that you establish honesty and communication with your child. It is difficult for a single parent to work, pay all the bills, and raise a child/children alone. It also becomes extremely important that you find some quality time for yourself and for your children. Parenting is a job within itself and trying to work and raise a child alone is twice as hard. If there is someone in your family or a friend that can help provide support, be open to allowing for help. Allow some quality time for yourself, even if it's a hot bubble bath and a good book while someone you trust and whom your children enjoy being with takes them out to the park or to get a hamburger. You need a couple hours here and there to gather your thoughts and relax. If you don't take this time for yourself then your frustration will continue to build and be taken out on your children. As a single parent, it is also important that you spend some quality time with your child/children and establish rapport and communication.

I hope that after reading this chapter, that you have realized the importance of using communication and consistency to establish and maintain mutual respect. Many families have told me, "We can't do this or that with our children because we can't financially afford it." Don't be afraid to have fun with your child. Take time out of your busy schedule and spend some quality time. Work and bills will still be there when you return. Set it aside, reduce your stress, and spend time with your kids. Going to the park or throwing a ball, etc. does not cost money. Be creative and allow your child to come up with ideas of things you can do together. One example of creative time is to turn on the radio and sing and dance with your child. This activity costs nothing but your time, and it can provide fun and laughter and may even lower your own stress level. Raising a child to have respect and the ability to communicate effectively, along with taking care of both you and your child's emotional health does not cost anything financially. It comes from your intrinsic desires and abilities. Remember those intrinsic desires are truth, love and acceptance. They don't cost money, they just enhance your relationship and provide quality time with your child—time you will not get back once they grow up. So I say to you, how can you not afford it?

10 Wants vs. Needs

This chapter is to motivate you to think about the concept of wants and needs. Webster's Dictionary (1999), defines the word *want* as "a wish or desire, to feel that one would like to have, do, or get." It defines the word *need* as "something that one wants or must have, a condition that makes something necessary."

Our basic *needs* are food, shelter, and clothing. I want to take *need* a step further, to remind you that we also *need* love, respect, acceptance and nurturing. However, a lot of us *want* much more in life. We 'want' that shiny, new car. We 'want' more money. We 'want' that $200.00 pair of shoes. We 'want' the latest video game and gaming system, etc. When we speak of these types of *wants* we seem to speak of them in terms of *need*. We think we 'need' that shiny, new car. We think we 'need' that new pair of shoes, etc. In fact, we seem to be confusing our wants with our needs. We get so caught up in spending money on wants in an effort to stand out from the crowd, that we lose sight of what is truly important. We find ourselves in debt and spend all our time working to pay for our *wants*. We teach and role model this to our children, and then they become confused in regards to wants vs. needs, thus this vicious cycle continues. All the while, we have increased our stress level and have to work harder and longer hours to pay bills. The quality time with our family flies right out the window.

We get so caught up in the money trap and the rat race that we seem to forget about our actual needs and the needs of our children. Once you are in this cycle, you become a hamster on a wheel and continue to run harder and faster just to try and keep up. You become more stressed, more easily agitated, and you miss spending quality time with your children. "Life" and wants have gotten in the way and our actual needs toward positive nurturing, teaching and role modeling self-worth and acceptance has somehow gotten lost.

When we begin to speak in terms of 'want,' we fail to mention those things that we may 'need,' to feel better about ourselves. We have gotten to a place in society that to feel better about ourselves, we 'want' more money and the benefits that come with having more such as a new car, bigger home, etc. Sometimes we even supply our 'wants' with immediate gratification whether we have the money to afford it or not and we purchase things on credit. We have become a society that defines feeling good about ourselves by our material wealth and possessions. This is when we get our 'wants' confused with our 'needs.'

It is necessary to feel positive and good about ourselves. It is necessary for us to teach and role model positive things such as love, self-confidence, and acceptance to our children. This must come in the form of love, acceptance and nurturing. This has to be taught and role modeled; it cannot be bought. However, we've gotten confused along the way and feel the shiny, new possessions will help us to feel better about ourselves, get us noticed, give us confidence and make us who we are. We then teach and role model this type of thinking to our children.

For example, if we acquire a new possession to feel better about ourselves, what happens when the newness wears off? My guess is that we start back at square one and focus on obtaining something else to take its place. We desperately search for something to fill that void within us. We want something to help us to feel better about ourselves. In essence, this becomes a vicious cycle, and at the end of each cycle, we have not truly changed how we feel about ourselves and may have likely accrued more debt, worry, frustration, guilt and stress. Once this happens, where is our self-confidence, love and acceptance?

If you want positive change in your life and the lives of your children, stop chasing the all-mighty dollar and that *something* that is outside of you that you think will help you feel better about yourself. Remember, if you are living this way, you are role modeling and teaching this to your children. Begin to take a serious look at fulfilling your *needs* for food, shelter, clothing, love, respect, acceptance and nurturing. Once you get your life in perspective and understand the difference between needs and wants you will be able to save money and establish a healthier relationship with yourself and your family. Basically, this is about setting your priorities and doing what it takes to meet your needs and the needs of your family. Once you have done that, your wants may begin to change or at least not be so financially draining . You can then effectively role model and teach the positive things in life to your children because you are, in effect, living it. You will have more time to spend quality time with your children, and not be so stressed, frustrated or agitated when you do. Another reminder, if you are always stressed, frustrated and agitated, what are you role modeling and teaching your children?

If you accomplish the task of setting priorities, and establish love and respect within yourself and your home, you will find that other important aspects in your life will begin to open up for you. You will feel better about yourself and more confident in your decision making and parenting skills. You may even find new and exciting opportunities starting to arise. You will find that you will become more creative, energetic, and enthusiastic about your own life and the lives of your children. You will be able to allow yourself to operate outside of the blinders that so many of us wear. Then, instead of chasing the dollar and remaining in a cycle of debt, you will take control and manage the dollar. In turn, you will become a better manager of your own life and role model that to your children. This will build your self-esteem, your self-confidence and in turn allow you to role model these skills to your children. This will also allow you to be more involved in your child's life, activities, interests and education.

Our children have gotten confused about 'wants' and 'needs' and they learned it from us. During various times of the year, there is a new special toy that for whatever reason gets the media's attention. It becomes "the toy" our children want and think they must have. Is this "must have" toy a 'want' or a 'need?' If we get the toy, the child is happy; if we don't get the toy, the child is heartbroken. Now we're dealing with our child's feelings and beginning to confuse 'wants' and 'needs' again. Don't get me wrong, I'm not saying, don't buy your child toys. I'm using this as an example that we have bought into this confusion via media advertising and so have our children. Once again, as with our wants, the newness of the toy will wear off and then we're off to buy the next toy so our child will be happy again. We've missed the point of needs yet again and we remain in the cycle that material possessions will provide our happiness, our confidence, our love and acceptance, when, in fact, it does none of that. We must educate our children with love, acceptance and help to build their self-esteem. They need to learn the difference and understand that possessions are not the true key to happiness and self-esteem. However, many of us have not learned that concept as adults and we need to become aware of this before we can role model it to our kids. We have taught our children that their self-worth is based on what they have, wear, or possess.

As a society, we need to get back to understanding our basic needs to become truly happy. The needs come from within, and we must use our intrinsic desires and abilities to capture our needs to be happy with our family and ourselves. In other words, we all need love and respect, acceptance and nurturing. However, we must have love, acceptance and respect for ourselves to obtain and to share love, acceptance and respect with others. If you don't have love, acceptance and respect for yourself, how can you teach or role model it for your family? We should role model these needs to our children and allow them to love, accept, and respect themselves and others. We also need to help them enhance their creativity for their own emotional and educational growth. If we remain in the cycle of spending more and buying more, how can we help our children to learn creativity and self -acceptance? I have yet to witness a child that has received that "perfect toy" and use it toward fulfilling his/her 'need' or desire of self-worth and belonging. I have also yet to witness that shiny new car fulfill our 'need' or desires for self-worth and belonging. What we need to do is set our priorities, meet our personal 'needs,' and use our 'wants' as a reward for our positive personal growth.

11 Natural and Logical Consequences

I saved this chapter for last because I wanted you to have knowledge of the previous chapters and gain an understanding about how you can be more effective in your parenting skills. If you have gained a better awareness of your own behaviors and communication skills, then this chapter will help to finalize and "tidy up" what you have already obtained from this book.

This chapter is to help parents to identify appropriate consequences for behaviors. It also will help to instill a rewards system. It is our responsibility as adults and role models to help children grasp the concept of "right and wrong" and to learn that certain behaviors will have consequences or rewards. Earlier, I discussed positive and negative reinforcement. How you reinforce a child's behavior will make a difference. Sometimes we get so busy with life that we don't always pay attention to our children until something goes wrong, so don't get caught up in the consequence game and forget about the rewards. It is also our responsibility to establish a reward system and consistently reward or reinforce positive behavior. We can discipline a child in a number of ways that will help that child to recognize and practice learning to not make the same mistakes. As adults, we do not have to be controlling to get our point across to a child.

I have worked with numerous families over the years and realized that everyone has different skills and abilities that determine how they handle certain situations. Below is a list of various types of disciplinarians and parenting styles that I have encountered. Keep in mind this list is not all-inclusive, and it is only to provide you with education on various types of families and personalities. As you review these types of parenting styles, think about how a child's self-worth or self-esteem may be molded in this household.

Strict authoritarian: These people need to always be in control and seem to possess a superior attitude towards the child and others. They say things like, "you will do this, or else," or "you better OBEY me." (They may also have the "do as I say, not as I do" approach—this falls into the obey/control category and there is usually no room for positive teaching and role modeling)

Perfectionist: This parenting style is always demanding that the child perform up to the parent's expectations. The perfectionist seems to look for fault in the child and in those around them. He or she may have the attitude that no matter what others do, it is never good enough. The child usually feels they cannot be successful in anything they do or try for fear of not gaining acceptance from the parent.

Wishy/Washy: The wishy/washy parent has difficulty making decisions, and is afraid he or she will make a mistake. There is usually a lot of worry, stress and fear associated with this parenting style. They exhibit difficulty maintaining consistent rules and limits with the child and likely in their own life as well.

Love and Pity: They are usually very overprotective, spoils and/or may even shame the child. They may have difficulty remaining in their balance and swing from love to pity. They can be very critical of themselves, the child and/or others. They have the "life is not fair" or the "woe is me" mentality and may seek a lot of sympathy and attention from others. Their actions may also be based on using the word love to fit their needs and at other times they may become easily angered if things don't go their way. They want others to do things or expect the child to do things in the name of love and usually has conditions placed on their love. ("If you love me, you will... If you love me, I will....and you will...").

Responsible: This parent allows the child to make decisions, incorporates goals and believes in choices and limit setting. They educate and role model positive behaviors. They provide the child and others with respect. They understand the importance of maintaining an open line of communication within the home and take an active role in their child's life. They encourage respect and responsibility, but can also say "no" when necessary. This parent is usually open to further education and growth for themselves and the child.

This book is based on getting back to basics and understanding ourselves along with enhancing our awareness of those around us. This will help us, as parents and educators, to better understand why people and children, in particular, act and behave as they do. If we have this awareness, it can only benefit us to deal with situations more effectively.

Natural and logical consequences are consequences designed to help the child learn, and not to punish the child. An example that we've all experienced is: "don't touch the stove, it's hot and you'll get burned." The child goes ahead and touches the stove, and obviously, he or she gets burned. One important factor is to process with the child what he or she learned from touching the stove. Allow the child to communicate why he or she went ahead and touched the stove. Then process what the child learned from touching the stove, even after being told not to touch it. The natural and logical consequence for touching the stove is obviously pain and getting burned. You don't have to punish the child for going ahead and touching the stove.

Getting burned should be the natural and logical consequence for touching the stove. Maintaining understanding and open communication with your child during this process is key. Your child learns by this type of communication. Everyone has choices and everyone will experience a reward or consequence from that choice, whether positive or negative. The key is to allow the child to verbalize and gain an understanding of what was learned by the choice he or she made and to recognize if the choice arises again what would be the appropriate decision. This enhances their choices and decision-making skills.

Natural and logical consequences should be done within reason and make sense so that the child learns from his or her choices and actions. These consequences are used to help the child to become more aware in accepting responsibility for his or her own behavior. These consequences are not used to humiliate, confuse, or embarrass the child. Once the consequence has been given and completed, do not forget to process with the child about what he or she learned and what he or she can do differently the next time the situation arises. During the process time, the parent guides the child, but more importantly becomes an effective listener and communicator to the child. This enhances trust and acceptance. Help the child to identify his or her own alternatives and solutions as you help to guide him or her through the process. Help the child to understand whether the solutions and alternatives he or she identified may or may not work. This is a process of learning and helps him or her understand that when faced with choices he or she can learn to process what the results will be *before* the choice is made. This leads to them being able to think before they act on something.

I am enclosing some ideas to help you be creative in establishing and implementing natural and logical consequences. Consequences work differently for different people, and it is your responsibility to use trial and error to find what will work for your children. Remember that these consequences are not punishment, rather they are learning tools to help improve behaviors. When considering natural and logical consequences, keep the hot stove example in mind and keep the consequence simple so the child learns and understands.

Ideas for Natural and Logical Consequences Events and Consequences

Throwing rocks/toys
- Have to apologize
- Time out
- Process with parent/caregiver about why they chose to throw rocks or toys and what could have been the outcome of that choice; i.e.: (someone could get hurt, break a toy, etc. How would that make them *feel* if they hurt someone or broke a toy they really loved?)
- Allow the child to process choices and outcomes and feelings

Fighting
- Apologize
- Process with parent and peer about the anger and why they got in a fight
- Discuss what other alternatives they could have chosen, instead of fighting
- Discuss the feelings and the anger that led to them fighting

- Communicating and processing their feelings are vital
- Have both children that were involved in the fight to process other solutions and how they could have handled their anger or disagreement differently

Not listening
- Ask the child to repeat what is being said
- Possible time out or take some time to slow things down for a moment
- Process how the child feels when others won't listen to them. Then follow up with a discussion on how it makes you feel when the child does not listen to you
- Identify alternatives on how we can improve our listening skills and try to do better

As with these and any other examples you may come across, you can see that effective role modeling and communication along with processing feelings is imperative. This is how you teach and this is how you learn. You must allow your child to begin to come up with their own alternatives and solutions and guide them towards a better understanding and awareness. You've heard the statement: "out of the mouths of babes," so be aware that you may need to be open to making changes yourself as they discuss what they have seen you do or say. They may tell you that you did something to upset them, so take heed and do not get defensive. This is where both of you communicate and come up with alternatives and solutions to work together and to help each other. If you want them to do better, you will have to commit to do better.

This information is to provide you with ideas for implementing natural and logical consequences. The most important thing in setting limits and consequences is to process and help the child to understand what he or she has done along with gaining awareness how to not make the same mistake again. Helping them to understand effective choices and decision-making skills takes time and is always a learning and growing process. Remember to maintain awareness of your communication skills, because it will enhance gaining feedback from the child.

Another important factor in working with children is to provide them with two healthy choices when applicable. This allows them to learn to weigh their options in what they would rather do. For example, you can play with the toy or go on the swing with Mark, but you can't do both because it's almost time for supper. This provides the child with an opportunity to think about what he or she wants to do, and has to make a choice to do one or the other. This will also allow the child to accept responsibility for his or her own actions. For example, Bobby chose to play with the toy instead of playing on the swing with Mark. Now it's time to go inside, and Bobby gets upset because he didn't get to play and swing with Mark.

Process with Bobby that he made the choice to play with the toy and that it was his decision to do so. Maybe tomorrow, he can have the choice and opportunity to decide to play with Mark.

By using the above scenario you have given the child an opportunity to make his/her own choices. You have also helped the child to accept responsibility for the choice he or she has made, along with giving the child an opportunity to make a different choice for the following day.

When dealing with choices and consequences, sometimes we get so caught up in right and wrong, good and bad that we forget to implement a reward. Keep in mind that when your child is doing well rewards and praise are just as important if not more so than giving consequences. Start perceiving "the glass as half full instead of half empty." Find the good and expand on that to promote more positive responses and positive actions. As discussed earlier, positive reinforcement is imperative for a child that is doing well. As adults, if we constantly try to do well, and never receive any positive reinforcement for our actions and behaviors, we will likely stop trying. If the only type of attention or reinforcement we receive is for negative behaviors and actions, then we learn to act out negatively to receive some type of attention. This is called negative attention seeking or negative reinforcement. It is very important to maintain positive reinforcement for positive behaviors to keep from acting negatively in order to receive any type of attention.

In discussing choices, I would like to interject a segment from *The Resume of Life* (pages 126 – 127):

> "Like any parent, we don't always agree with the choices our kids make, but I've come to recognize, we cannot be with them 24/7 to make their choices for them. What we can do is model, teach, love and respect them. But we cannot hold on to, control or force them to be a certain way. As with energy, when you apply force, you will receive counterforce. Help them find, strengthen and maintain their internal sense of knowing. Help them to recognize those negative influences and forces that will come along during their journey. You are there to teach, to support, and work through their growing and learning processes. They need to be allowed to find their unique expression and build upon it. Teach them, model positivity for them, help them, support them but most of all: love and accept them for who they are."

I hope this book has provided you with insight into yourself, your partner, and your children. If we learn to listen to our heart and try to make the best choices and decisions that we can for our children, and for ourselves, then we will be successful. We all have trials and tests, and life is not always easy, but we have internal strength, desires and tools to get through whatever comes our way. You may not always like the choices and decisions your child makes for him/herself, but remember we are all human, and we all make choices in our lives that are sometimes not good for us, but hopefully we take the time to learn from those choices. When your child makes a mistake let him/her know that you may not be happy or like his/her behavior, but that does not mean you do not love him/her. However, if we learn to become capable of weighing our options, making the best choices and decisions possible, and accept responsibility for the consequences or rewards that come from that decision, then progress has been made.

Once again, I wish you the very best for yourself and your family while on your parenting journey.

Namaste my friend, Namaste!

Terry J. Walker, M.A.

About the Author

Terry began her career working as a probation officer for adolescents in the community. She provided intensive probation, individual and family counseling. She also helped to develop a program for children and teens in the community in an effort to give kids alternatives to getting into trouble.

She later worked inpatient Dual Diagnosis and became a Program Director for a long term residential treatment center providing individual, group and family therapy.

She developed a program for daycares and early childhood education teachers to "bridge the gap" between early childhood educators and parents. Terry's mission for *Bridging the Gap* is to enhance children's behavioral skills and educational abilities along with implementing mutual awareness and communication between families and educators.

Over the past 14 years she has also worked in medical sales and customer service industry where she also provided motivational sales and customer service training techniques to colleagues and clients.

During her journey, she, like you encountered numerous successes and pitfalls and has taken the time to try and "figure it out." She now wants to share her insight with you.

Terry holds a Master of Arts Degree in Educational Psychology and Counseling from Tennessee Tech University, and a Bachelor of Science Degree in Mass Communications from Middle Tennessee State University.

Terry is a business owner (Inspire and Motivate, IAM) and motivational speaker. Her other books include: *Bridging the Gap: An Educator's Guide,* and *The Resume of Life, A Guide to Realizing Your Purpose Through Spirit, Mind and Body.*

To invite Terry to inspire and motivate your group at your next event, contact her at: terry@iamterryjwalker.com or visit her website: IAMTerryJWalker.com.